YOU COULD
LOSE AN EYE

YOU COULD LOSE AN EYE

My first eighty years in Montreal

By David Reich

Baraka
Books

Montreal

Cover by Folio Infographie
Illustration by David Reich
Book design by Folio Infographie

Legal Deposit, 4th quarter, 2010
Bibliothèque et Archives nationales du Québec
Library and Archives Canada

Published by Baraka Books of Montreal.
6977, rue Lacroix
Montréal, Québec H4E 2V4
Telephone: 514 808-8504
info@barakabooks.com
www.barakabooks.com

Printed and bound in Quebec

Trade Distribution & Returns

Canada:
LitDistCo
1-800-591-6250; orders@litdistco.ca

United States:
Independent Publishers Group
1-800-888-4741 (IPG1);
orders@ipgbook.com

NOTE

The title of this Memoir, *You could lose an eye*, was an urgent warning Ma always issued when I was about to embark on any hazardous undertaking: playing hockey, swinging a bat, riding a bicycle... our world was filled with high-risk activities that included almost everything except doing homework, playing chess, or competing at Monopoly. It was an expression of her love and concern.

These chapters recall aspects of my life and of those who gave it meaning. Memories are ephemeral. They sometimes fade, or transform themselves. I tried to be exact and truthful; if errors have intruded, or if I have wrongly judged anyone, I am truly sorry. Any mistakes were unintentional; nothing was dictated by malice,

I have freely resorted to Yiddish to better transmit the flavour of my environment and include a GLOSSARY for those less fluent in my *momeh loshen* [mother tongue].

This book could never have been written without the enthusiastic co-operation of many family members and friends. Ma's sister, Miriam Ivry Reich—one hundred years old in spring 2011—took time from her bridge group to recall four generations of family lore; cousins Judy Geiger, Danny Reich, and Mark Reich provided a wealth of oral history dictated by Pa's brother, Nathan, featured here as The Professor. Another cousin, Miriam Brahms Reich, my aunt Lisl Ivry, my brother Lionel, and many others found rare letters, photos, and documents from the family's past. Miriam and Lisl also permitted use of excerpts from poignant memoirs recounting their wartime experiences.

I am indebted to Miriam Roland, who tirelessly edited my drafts and struggled with its imperfections, and to family members who patiently submitted to my interviews, examined the text, and made valuable corrections and comments. No doubt further information will be forthcoming. God willing, I'll be around to revise and correct my story.

On the running board, circa 1930, with grandmother Chaya Tzipporah (Yavorovitz) Ivry lurking in the background.

CONTENTS

DEDICATION

This is the story of my family.

I lovingly dedicate it to my Ma and Pa who came to Canada in the 1920s and to those of our *mishpocha* who remained in Europe and perished in the Holocaust. I never saw my paternal grandparents or the families that died with them, never heard their voices, and never embraced them. They died as strangers, yet they live inside me. I must keep their memories alive. They persisted in their faith through the centuries, leading decent, honourable lives. Beset by poverty, prejudice, and lack of opportunity, they continued to aspire.

This is not an autobiography. Readers expecting high drama, thrilling events, or lurid confessions will be disappointed. The persons populating this book are ordinary folk whose lives, although not sensational, deserve what little immortality these pages can bring.

This story is especially directed to the fine children I raised: Jonathan, Dahlia, Paul, Errol, Ingrid, and Jenny; to the wonderful children they, in turn, now raise; Alexander, Noah, Jonas, Joshua, Truman, Graeme, Eli, Madeline, Gabrielle, Gabriel, Jamie, Sabrina, Rachel, and Lucy—and those who may follow.

I write so they will not be as ignorant of my life and times as I am of my own grandparents and those who preceded them. These lives have meaning and passing generations should take note of them; they are all part of us.

PART 1

MY FIRST 80 YEARS...

MA AND PA

Putting Down Roots

At the turn of the twentieth century, Emperor Franz Josef reigned over the Austria-Hungarian Empire, Tsar Nicholas ruled Russia, and Kaiser Wilhelm was master of Germany. From the safety of their palaces these intrepid monarchs sent millions to their deaths in the First World War. The resulting upheaval encouraged millions to migrate to a "new world." They travelled light: their only baggage was intelligence, energy, and burning ambition. It was more than enough.

Many arrived in Canada, profoundly grateful to have arrived anywhere. Among them were a couple of *Galizianers*, Hirsch (anglicized to Harry) Reich, and his older brother, Mordkhe (Marcus). A younger brother, Nute (Nathan), landed in 1923. They had been born in Terszow, a backwater village in Galicia, an insignificant corner of the Ukraine. In 1920, they became Montrealers.

At about the same time, Genya Ivry (Jennie) arrived from Vilkaviskis, Lithuania, one of a wave of Jewish immigrants identified as *Litvacks*. She was greeted by her father, Avrum Leib. His three brothers had landed in America early in the twentieth century and he had taken their mother to visit them. Attracted to the "new world," he returned to settle in Montreal in 1911, expecting to send for his family. The First World War intervened; only in 1923 was he reunited with his wife, Chaya Tzipporah, his daughter Miriam and his son, Sidney. Two other sons, Harold and Sol, daughters, Leah (married to Moe Blostein), and Sochie (married to Yosef Rabin) joined them later. By 1929 the Ivry family was settled in Montreal, except for the Rabin ménage; they nested in Ottawa, but they might just as well lived next door.

Harry Reich was destined to be my Pa; Jennie Ivry became my Ma. This is their story—and mine.

★ ★ ★

Jennie and Harry met at the Baron de Hirsch Institute where they had come to learn their new language. They found more in common than a desire to master English and, over their grammar texts, friendship blossomed into love. A faded invitation records that their wedding was fixed for January 11, 1925, at the New Adath Jeshurun Synagogue on Mount Royal Boulevard, to be followed by a reception at 81 Villeneuve West. Pa was twenty-seven years old, Ma a couple of years older. The wedding portrait shows him standing handsomely erect in a tuxedo, a carnation in his lapel. His abundant hair was combed straight back from his forehead and he sported a discreet moustache; both disappeared with age. A slender Ma sat beside him in a pleated white gown with a gossamer tulle veil stretching from a beribboned headpiece into a train piled artistically at her feet. A bouquet nested on her lap; she never looked more regal. Both were serious and purposeful, calm in the face of challenges to come—like royalty, not at all like a couple of immigrants five years off the boat. I, their crown prince, was born two years later; the dynasty was launched.

The synagogue and the Reich flat were in the heart of Montreal's ghetto, an area where two- and three-storey shabby, undersized, under-heated apartment buildings crowded against each other, their dimly lit rooms looking into air shafts or courtyards or back alleys. They were reached by outside stairways that twisted to their upper floors: obstacle courses in summer and bobsled runs during the long, dark, icy winters.

But this ghetto didn't bear the stigma and isolation of its European counterparts. It teemed with Jews from every European hovel, happy to be safe and surrounded by their own people in a neighbourhood in which the language and signs were Yiddish and energies could be devoted to making a living and raising children to be real Canadians and good Jews. They were breathing free air after centuries of subsisting in wretched villages and confronting

Ma and Pa (Jennie and Harry Reich) were married in Montreal on January 11, 1925.

pogroms, drunken peasants and rapacious officials. In due course the problems of these impoverished communities were settled by the Final Solution. They would send no more Jews.

My father and mother stemmed from different milieus. Lithuanian Jews (*Litvacks*) considered themselves superior in education, in the quality of the Yiddish they spoke, and in all matters cultural. Galician Jews (*Galizianer*) were more pious and regarded *Litvacks* as virtual non-believers: they lisped and lived on herring—sources of merriment, if not derision. Despite these critical differences, my Ma and Pa remained together until parted by death after half a century of marriage.

Language, except for English, was not a problem. Living on frontiers of Europe's unstable, racially diverse countries had made them polyglots. Ma had studied French in the *gimnasium*, learned Swedish while caring for children in Sweden and could communicate in ten languages. Pa was close behind. Initially, the language at our home was Yiddish. My parents quickly acquired an accented English. Mothers or fathers without Old World accents were unknown in our neighbourhood and a British accent was equated with membership in the royal family. Grandparents rocked in chairs, covered their heads with *shaitels* or *yarmulkes*, and praised, chastised, gossiped, and instructed in pure Yiddish until they passed on leaving us their incomparable heritage.

The Yiddish that we imbibed with mother's milk was the richest and most eloquent of languages: warm, comfortable, and infinitely expressive of the Jewish soul. It verbalized the misery of life in exile, the voice of a people coping with oppression, surviving, and keeping their faith—if not in humanity, then in God. Its bittersweet humour and its sadness and pathos, born of persecution, massacres, and expulsions, could not be defined in dictionaries. It needed the speaker's tongue, hands, and shoulders and included shrugs, smiles, scowls, winks, lifted eyebrows, intonations, eloquent silences, and cryptic idioms, all beyond linguistic description. The pompous were pricked, fools were exposed, hypocrites were mocked, and the haughty were derided. It is no accident that this language, and the culture that it reflected, so strongly influenced American humour and drama. My English was acquired on the street and polished in the classroom. I write in English, but my mind and spirit spring directly from my *momeh loshen* that resonates in me.

Ma and Pa had unknowingly landed in Quebec. They weren't aware that the province was dominated by French-speaking Catholics with a sprinkling of Anglo-Saxon Protestants diluted by a mix of Europeans. For us, French, lingua franca for eighty percent of the population, was a foreign tongue, only another school course, less important than arithmetic and history. It never entered our minds that it would become an imperative in our later years. We could successfully ignore the French- and English-speaking neighbours alike, except when we were chased by *shkotzim* intent on seeking revenge for the son of God, whose image, impaled on crosses, stared accusingly down on us in every room in every public building.

We had no gentile friends. We weren't prejudiced, we didn't know them; we were from different worlds. We bought from them, sold to them, but never interacted socially, in or out of our homes. It wasn't forbidden—we simply had nothing in common with them, nothing to say to each other. We were a race apart. Our relationship only thawed decades later.

Our family was more than closely knit; it was woven, meshed, and glued. Ma took over the life of each arriving family member. Marcus, Pa's brother who had arrived in Montreal with him, welded the family together even more by marrying Ma's youngest sister, Miriam, in 1936. Why start a family with a stranger? They had two children, Harriet (Susi) and Lawrence, my double cousins.

Another of Ma's siblings, Leah, had married a Jewish teacher before arriving in Canada. Moe Blostein was well qualified: like Ma, he was from Lithuania, an intellectual with opinions on every subject that he was ready to discuss at length between puffs on Turkish cigarettes. He prefaced every argument by intoning "And I'll tell you something else..." followed by an exposition from behind his Turkish smoke screen. Ma, an ardent nepotist, had already conscripted her three brothers, Harold, Sol, and Sidney, into Pa's business, but there was room for the new brother-in-law. Moe became manager.

During the 1930s Pa managed to extract two nephews, Herman Reich and Henry Narzisenfeld (Field), from Poland. Then Canada's iron gates clanged shut; Jews were excluded. As an anonymous Canadian immigration agent elegantly put it, "None is too many."[1] Those remaining in Galicia, Pa's parents, brother, sisters, their spouses and offspring, were murdered and bulldozed into unmarked ditches.

Herman and Henry joined the family in what we called The Store. My brother Lionel was also drafted, and Marcus's son, Lawrence, a fledgling lawyer, met a similar fate. I was never drawn into the business, preferring the hardships and satisfactions of an architectural career. It was also more fun.

---

1. Quoted in Irving Abella and Harold Troper, *None Is Too Many: Canada and the Jews of Europe 1933–1948* (Toronto: Lester & Orpen Dennys, 1983).

Moe Blostein and
Ma's sister Leah and
their niece Esther circa
1926. Leah died in
1933 and their baby
son Maier was raised
by Ma and Pa.

Sadly, Leah died young from a disease so fearsome that its name
was never mentioned. When questioned on the cause of death the
family's invariable response was *"freg nisht."* Another dreaded diag-
nosis was *"zog nisht."* When I heard these sentences pronounced, I
knew that a funeral would shortly follow. (Years later, I discovered
that these were family euphemisms for cancer.) Leah left a year-old
son Maier. Moe was told by Ma that his son should be raised within
a family and he was transferred to our home. My Pa became his and
Moe became an uncle who, like all other uncles, aunts, and cousins
had unlimited visiting rights that came with the privilege of having
their destinies shaped by Ma. He grew up to be a professor at McGill
University and director of Bell Telephone Laboratories. Possessing
the Ivry's musical gene, he taught himself to play piano.

★ ★ ★

It would be an exaggeration to say that we were welcomed, loved, or joyfully accepted in Quebec. Obstacles were everywhere and discrimination abounded. There were no pogroms, but anti-Semitism was alive and well. Our family business was on a street lined with Jewish-owned businesses. They dealt with banks whose windows carried Yiddish signs that not one of their gentile employees could read. Financial institutions were *Judenrein*; Jews had no place in insurance companies, public utilities, and countless private firms. Our district schools, filled almost entirely with Jewish students, employed only English-speaking Protestants. No teachers of the Hebrew faith were accepted. McGill University, prestigious dispenser of degrees, required Jewish applicants to have ten percent higher matriculation marks than non-Jews and some faculties imposed quotas. Resort hotels carried signs: *No Jews or Dogs*. I wondered what they had against dogs. They'd never crucified anyone. There was a precedent: Jesus' family was refused shelter in an inn and consigned to a manger. But for us there were no vacancies, not even in their mangers.

In certain districts, title deeds prohibited property sales to Jews; in others, Jewish students were excluded from schools until legislation was passed. Jewish doctors were not accepted into hospitals; in response, we built our own Jewish General Hospital. Jews were excluded from many private clubs devoted to golf, curling, tennis, yachting, and just plain socializing. In response, we created the Elmridge Golf Club, the Greystone Curling Club, the Lord Reading Yacht Club, and the Montefiore Club, where we could play cards, enjoy cocktails, smoke cigars and celebrate family occasions in tuxedos—almost as if we were gentiles.

Yet Ma and Pa were grateful to be allowed to live in Canada, where we could walk in safety. Pictures of the king and queen hung on our walls as our personal saviours. By accepting us as Canadians, the royal family had saved us from the endless pogroms and vicious anti-Semitism of Eastern Europe and reprieved us from the Holocaust. We were well aware that we were not favoured by the local gentiles, but we knew that their feelings and actions were nothing compared to those that poisoned the countries that Ma and Pa had left.

For the less attractive elements of our lives, Ma and Pa had a simple answer to Christian benevolence: work harder, faster, smarter. We did—and we prospered.

Raising Children

On September 17, 1927, ten pounds of solid flesh were delivered at the Royal Victoria Hospital. I was the first member of our family born in Canada. In recognition of my sturdy physique I was called the "policeman of the ward." Possibly because countless generations of my forefathers had lived impoverished lives in Eastern European *shtetls*, I emerged hungry, an ominous portent for my future life. It stayed with me.

Rabbi Colton, Montreal's most prolific *mohel*, presided over my public debut at my circumcision. He presented my parents with an impressive photographic affidavit, devoted mostly to his bearded visage, attesting to my birth and his handiwork. This was my religious and civil birth certificate and for decades I was obliged to present his imposing portrait to any official whom I had to convince that I existed. I did so with my face averted and my cap pulled down as far as my nose permitted. It certified that I had been born and circumcised; only my foreskin was missing from the document. I discovered sixty years later that my birth date was incorrect; I was actually one day younger than advertised, a circumstance that caused endless confusion in my later life as driver's permits, passports, credit cards, and medical records required correction, a task that baffled guardians of these vital records. That discrepancy of a single day created employment for an army of clerks.

My brother Lionel followed three years later. He was smaller than I and suffered less from hunger pangs. But he was prone to ear infections, a serious matter in those pre-antibiotics days. He needed protection.

Lionel and I got on well. Because I was bursting with good health, exuberance, and independence, I was sent to summer camps. Lionel, suspected of frailties, was more tied to Ma's apron strings. Being younger, his arrival in school was always greeted by, "Oh, you're David's brother." Unfortunately, he was judged by my boisterous performance.

Telephone Belair 2155-F

Rabbi J. L. COLTON

PRACTICAL MOHEL
And Marriage Performer

4867 ESPLANADE AVE.
MONTREAL, Canada

טעלעפאָן בעלעיר 2155-עף

הרב י. ל. קאָלטאָהו

מוהל
ומסדר קדושין

4867 עספלאָנייד עװ.
מאָנטרעאל, קענעדע.

שם הילד 3/3

נולד ביום _____ לחודש _____ שנת תר"פ _____ נמול ביום _____ לחודש _____ תר"פ

שם אביו _____ שם אמו _____

Name of the child *David*

Born *September 17-* 192*7*

Day of Circumcision *September 24-th 1927*

Father's Name *Harry Reich*

Mother's Name *Jennie Swry*

Address: *5602 Parke ave. Montreal Cana*

Reg'd. by the Congregation *Chemerin Labeker*

Rabbi *J. L. Colton*

Montreal's most prolific Mohel, well known for his handiwork.

In the absence of any strong alternative inclination, Lionel cut short his formal education and was swept into the family business that the world knew as Reich Brothers Limited and that we knew as The Store. Lionel had a gift for languages and a taste for exposition. He could have been a successful pedagogue. In addition to Yiddish and French, he studied Hebrew, Aramaic, Arabic, German, and Italian. But he was imprisoned in The Store and spent the rest of his working life in a business for which he had no love and little talent. He persevered, but the market changed; Reich Brothers Limited didn't. Lionel presided over its demise toward the turn of the century and gratefully retired. A load was lifted from his shoulders.

He winters in one of Florida's Century Villages. When not discussing the world affairs around the pool with his fellow statesmen, he takes tennis lessons, and, being the only Reich with any musical aptitude, plays the accordion, studies piano, and aspires to song writing. In Montreal, he occupies spare moments with three grandchildren. It suits him well; he is content.

My life was not entwined with Lionel's. I had my own friends and interests. I read voraciously. A handsomely bound twenty-volume set of the Books of Knowledge entranced me for a decade. I lost myself in translations of thousand-page novels by Victor Hugo, Eugene Sue, Leo Tolstoy, and Fyodor Dostoevsky. By flashlight, instead of sleeping, I salivated over risqué stories by Guy de Maupassant and Honoré de Balzac, shivered over terror tales by Edgar Allan Poe, and marvelled at Jules Verne's fantasies. I perished heroically on bobbing ice floes with every Arctic and Antarctic explorer. I was caned at British public schools in the pulp magazines *Champion* and *Triumph* and then strolled through British society with Somerset Maugham, John Galsworthy, and Charles Dickens. I savoured the sharp wit of Oscar Wilde, Dorothy Parker, and George Kaufman. I suffered with Israel Joseph Singer and Israel Zangwill in ramshackle *shtetls* from which Ma and Pa had fled. My world had no limits. I came by literature honestly. Ma, an avid Russophile, filled me with Russian romances: tales of passion and magnificent spectacles in which nobles danced the night away in the arms of their lovers, against a background of assassinations and revolutions.

And history! I conquered the world with the Romans, fought hand-to-hand in every war with armies of every nation. I sang La Marseillaise in front of the Bastille during the French revolution, dodged bullets as the Russians revolted in Petrograd, charged with the Light Brigade at Balaclava, and was the sole survivor of the siege of Khartoum and the massacre of the Alamo. I passed a glorious, bloodthirsty and inspiring childhood totally safe in my warm, comfy bed where I couldn't lose an eye.

Although my real life was nowhere near as dramatic, I recall some exciting episodes.

The family spent several weeks every summer in a rented cottage near a beach. Ma could sit in comfort and supervise her brood, occasionally taking to the water to dunk herself up to her armpits. Those were refreshing and carefree times. One ambitious summer we travelled to Old Orchard, a vacation town in Maine with a vast sandy expanse fronting on a vaster sea. I was about seven years old and had developed some independence; I disappeared. For six frantic hours the family searched for me; they were ready to drag the entire Atlantic Ocean. I was found that evening in a roller-skating rink. Recriminations followed. It was the last summer I accompanied the family on a holiday. Thereafter I was banished to summer camps in the Laurentian Mountains. It was easier to drag a lake.

The war started the year I turned twelve. It brought changes: travel was restricted because of gas rationing, security regulations were imposed, and harbours and military airports were sealed off. A new airport located in the Montreal suburb of Dorval was the base from which bombers flew to England. It was all very secret. About this time I acquired a bicycle and loved exploring the countryside around Montreal, following narrow winding roads past vegetable farms that have long since been swallowed up in the city's expansion. One of these byways ran along the perimeter of Dorval Airport. Beyond a chain-link fence protecting its boundary I could see bombers awaiting delivery to the battlefront. It was incredibly exciting. Exercising unusually poor judgment, I lay my bicycle down, climbed a grassy embankment, and wiggled under a loose section of the fence; I was among these massive aircraft. I wandered about, examining them, but not for long. I was arrested. It didn't help that my name was Reich. After questioning, however, even my captors recognized that I was no security risk and a couple of phone calls confirmed my identity. Instead of facing a firing squad, I had to face Pa; it was not an easy choice. Mercifully, he had a few words for me, but, at least, I could walk away.

I was not always a troublemaker; once, I was a hero. Ma and Pa went to visit friends one evening, leaving me in charge of the house. Maier had lost a toy under a sofa and lit a match to search for it. The fabric ignited. I smelled smoke and entered the room just as flames reached the curtains. I pulled them down and phoned the fire department. Unwilling to make a fuss, I explained we had only a small blaze and not to hurry. Within minutes they arrived, doused the flames, and threw the smouldering sofa onto the snow-covered lawn, greatly surprising my returning parents. I didn't get a medal, but, even better: Ma and Pa were proud of me.

Although I gave Ma much to complain about, lack of appetite was not one of my failings. Throughout my formative years, I never heard the word *nutrition*. Diets were for the sick, imposed by solemn professionals who were themselves living skeletons, never having enjoyed a good meal throughout their entire tortured existences. In Europe rich men and women were expected to be portly; their substance confirmed their wealth. Thin folk were suspected of having tuberculosis, then called consumption. I wondered why; surely it was due to *lack* of consumption.

I knew nothing of vitamins, minerals, or supplements. How could one supplement hearty beef, fat chickens, fresh vegetables, or luscious fruit? What did one need besides pickles, sauerkraut, and coleslaw? Why would one resist rich chocolate cake or flaky-crusted pie stuffed with apples liberally coated with cinnamon? Ma served real food, not fibre, protein, and carbohydrates. No pre-cooked foods entered our home; everything was made by Ma. Cholesterol hadn't been invented. I never saw a sweetener, colorant, enhancer, or trace element, or heard of additives. And my system never lacked boron, zinc, chromium, iron, iodine, or anything else. She spiced my meals with garlic and didn't skimp on oil or vinegar. My healthy ignorance of nutrition permitted me to enjoy a long and rewarding career.

My Ma

Ma was one of seven children of the Ivry family from Vilkaviskis, Lithuania, then a province of Imperial Russia. The father, Avrum Leib, had arrived in Montreal three years before the Russian Tsar and the Austria-Hungarian Emperor decided to have a war.

It started in 1914. As the German army advanced over the frontier and occupied their town, the Ivry family prudently sought refuge further east, in Vilna. When that city was also taken, they returned home—except Ma. She'd found employment as a governess with a family. They moved to Sweden and she spent her next five years in Stockholm before coming to Canada in 1920.

★ ★ ★

I was raised by my Ma. My Pa was chained to The Store, working to sustain us. He left the house before we were awake and returned after we'd eaten supper. By then, he was too tired and too distracted to involve himself in our homework, to inquire about school, friends or activities. More intimate contact was reserved for weekends, when we might walk together, or enjoy a modest family outing. But we knew Pa was there, something like a Deity who hovered over us, invisible but worshipped: his approval was important. But our daily lives were directed by Ma.

She was a homemaker, preparing and transforming what was needed for our sustenance. Wine bubbled on the back balcony, cucumbers and tomatoes soured in the pantry, brisket and tongue pickled in the refrigerator, and fat herrings covered with onions ripened in spiced brine. Berries were turned to jam and fruit became marmalade. We feasted on schmaltz (chicken fat) with griben (fried chicken fat) that melted into rye bread and, basking in our ignorance, we swallowed unhatched chicken eggs in rich chicken soup. We devoured these delicacies not because we were greedy, but in gratitude for living in a land of plenty; it was our obligation, one that we took seriously. Ma constantly admonished me, "Eat. They're starving in India. In China is a famine. In Armenia is nothing but skin and bones." I left nothing on my plate except the cutlery; I will retain the flesh I acquired until I'm carried to my final destination, leaving the pallbearers to struggle with my remains.

Ma's meals required lengthy preparation and deserved serious gustatory attention; any food left uneaten attracted prompt investigation. "The brisket is too tough? Oy, Sidney, that *goniff* of a butcher! Here, try the chicken." But, in fact, Sydney was not a thief, but an honest tradesman whose weekly deliveries I hold accountable for a considerable portion of my bulk. Our family was nourished for decades by his *mittlechock*, *leber*, *brisket*, and other portions of bovine anatomy, not to mention his lamb, chickens, turkeys, and geese.

Every Monday Ma berated him as she gave her order and every Thursday he delivered, with a smile, a heavy parcel, covered with wax paper and plastered with blood-soaked newsprint from the Montreal Star, containing, he swore, the freshest, leanest beef and the fattest fowl that felt privileged to be slaughtered to nourish the Reich family.

Unfailingly, every Sunday with unerring timing, in the middle of a vast meal featuring his livestock transformed into a banquet fit for Henry VIII, the doorbell would ring. Sidney the *Goniff* was collecting for his carnivorous offerings. He would shuffle into the dining room carrying the same stub of an indelible pencil behind his ear since the start of his butchering career. It seemingly lasted forever.

Ma would give him a piece of her mind: *Sidney, you Goniff, the veal you sent me was nothing but fat, your chicken, nebich, had starved to death, your mittelchock....* and so on.

Undeterred by pieces of Ma's mind, he listened. He'd lick the flattened lead tip of that pencil stub and total up hieroglyphics tattooed in a notebook of tangled leaves of carbon paper. Ma assembled the requisite sum to the penny, expressing the fervent hope that, starting next week, his food would meet minimum standards of edibility. Sidney wrote PAID IN FULL, returned the pencil to his ear and swore to provide full satisfaction. He did, for thirty years. He eventually retired to collect rents from apartments purchased with his blood money.

Before Ma honoured Sidney with her patronage, she shopped at a local butcher whose meat was certified kosher. I loved to accompany her; it was my favourite shop, smelling of raw meat that oozed blood onto the sawdust-covered floor. The man at the counter took orders from housewives who jostled each other like vultures feeding on carrion, while butchers flashed their knives against steel sharpening rods and hacked, sawed, and sliced flesh and bones from honest-to-goodness carcasses of cows and lambs that swung gently on hooks. Chickens hanging by their scrawny necks were beheaded with a single swift stroke, deftly dismembered and wrapped in wax paper with their neck, legs, liver, and unhatched eggs. When Ma was satisfied with her bloody booty, we left the store, brushing the sawdust from our shoes.

Ma would complete the butchering, removing pinfeathers, and trimming, salting, grinding, chopping or slicing beast and fowl as her time-honoured recipes required. Her knives were almost as sharp as the butcher's—and why not? Didn't a skilled sharpener roll his portable stand down the street, ringing his bell to alert every Ma in the neighbourhood that her knives and scissors were dull and needed attention from his grindstones? He rang his bell loudly, he was at the doorstep and his fees were modest; there was no excuse for dull blades.

Ma cooked, sewed, darned, laundered, and cleaned until we could afford a maid. What she couldn't do, she organized and supervised. In pre-refrigerator days, hefty deliverymen stumbled up our stairs lugging giant tongs pinching ice blocks that they slid into our wooden icebox. This ingenious food-cooling system was environmentally perfect: the unit used no electricity and was biodegradable, ice froze naturally in the St. Lawrence River, and the only moving parts were the ice deliverymen and a bottom pan that Ma emptied. She scrubbed soiled clothes by hand over a corrugated washboard, squeezed them through a wringer, and attached them with wood pegs to clotheslines that hung like spider webs over back yards where they flapped in the wind, acquiring an aroma never matched by modern dryers or chemical fresheners. Furnaces burned coal stored in a cellar; their ashes were spread over the outside stairs and driveways in winter to ensure non-slip surfaces. In most apartment buildings garbage was dropped through chutes into incinerators that converted waste into noxious fumes that blanketed the city, competing with oil-laden breezes blowing from the east-end refineries.

Ma never rested, managing the home as capably as Pa managed the business. Not a penny was wasted, not a morsel of food thrown out; a compost heap would have waited in vain for anything more substantial than egg shells from our table. Nor would we have needed a recycling container; newspapers and string were collected for packaging at The Store and containers were salvaged for Ma's endless variety of homemade jams, biscuits, preserves, and soups. Our home was immaculate; it was Ma's domain. Pa never washed or even carried a dish, or shovelled ash, or watered a plant, or changed a diaper. The Store was Pa's empire. The boundaries were clear. There was never an argument; it was a seamless partnership.

Ma was the unquestioned family matriarch by seniority and personality. She wasn't arrogant; the mantle of divine right rested naturally on her shoulders. Her sovereignty extended over Pa, her children, her brothers and sisters, and those whom they married. She dominated by sheer force of will, never raising her voice. It wasn't necessary. She turned on her subjects with gimlet eyes that flanked an imperious Roman nose and pronounced judgment quietly, with authority. There was no dissent. We all understood our places.

★ ★ ★

Although strict, Ma had her kindly side. She admired culture, learning, integrity, and quietly befriended many less fortunate than her. It would have been an insult to make this known. Among them was Miss Wiseberg. If Miss Wiseberg had a first name, we never knew it. All eighty pounds of her, assembled along the lines of a sparrow, bespoke miss. She was unique among Ma's friends because of her distinguished British accent, and was, in fact, a private teacher of English, mostly to recent immigrants. In those depression years, schoolteachers barely made a living and any other kind lived on, or over, the brink of starvation.

Miss Wiseberg was elderly, but ageless, with the faded elegance of withered gentility. My mother welcomed her as a fellow aristocrat and they sipped tea and chatted for an afternoon every week. Their conversations, about books, music, and history, were intimate and subdued. As supper hour approached, Miss Wiseberg would stir, as if to leave. This was the signal for Ma to start in surprise at the passing time and the following conversation ensued almost word for word over the many years that she shared our lives.

"Miss Wiseberg, you must stay for supper!"

"Oh, Genya, I couldn't put you to the trouble."

"Trouble? What trouble? Where trouble? I am insulted that you leave without eating."

From her appearance, Miss Wiseberg hadn't had a square meal that week. Needless to say she stayed and, between my Ma and her friends, she survived unchanged for decades.

Time took its toll and Miss Wiseberg slipped into sickness. I was delegated to move her from the single room that she rented to an even smaller and poorer alcove that she occupied between trips to the hospital. The whole of her belongings fitted into her cardboard valise that I carried as she chirped on in her British accent, every inch a lady. There was never a complaint, never a reference to her long life unfilled by husband or children, or to her lingering and finally fatal illness.

She died as she lived, respected and sustained by Ma and others who valued her company. No doubt, after being suitably persuaded, she is at this very moment sitting at God's table, murmuring in refined British tones over her tea. God probably addresses her as Miss Wiseberg. Even He doesn't know her first name.

* * *

But family wasn't treated as indulgently. Our lives were grist for Ma's comments: buying a fur coat; renting or purchasing a dwelling; choosing friends or schools. Nothing escaped her. She was achievement-oriented and strict, with no latitude for nonsense or excuses. It wasn't necessary to ask her opinion; it was freely given. For better or worse, Ma was my role model for every female I later encountered. Age and illness diminished her influence, but she remained a force until her last breath.

Ma was not demonstrative. She didn't envelop us with hugs or smother us with wet kisses. She didn't sigh lovingly when we returned from school; she didn't dither, she was all business: "Drink your milk. Eat your cake. Do your homework." Pampering wasn't a family failing. But we lacked for nothing.

We never heard the words "style" or "fashion." Everyone in the neighbourhood dressed alike. Clothes had to be warm and service-able: thick wool stockings, indestructible corduroy pants leather-trimmed at vulnerable junctions, shoes with triple-thickness soles bearing a lifetime guarantee against flexing, snug mittens whose elastic cuffs ensured a tourniquet fit at the wrists, padded caps with earflaps. I could have comfortably survived on the moon or trekked to the South Pole. We had what we needed—that was all. It never entered our minds to ask for more.

★ ★ ★

Shopping for shoes was an event. Once a year we went to Eaton's, the largest and grandest department store in Montreal. It reeked of competence, its staff was knowledgeable, and its service was flaw-less. They had to be: Eaton's promised *Goods Satisfactory or Money Refunded*. Shopping there was no mad dash of acquisition but a measured and time-honoured ritual. When I needed new shoes we went to see Monsieur Malette. Among his attractions was the store escalator that whisked us to the mezzanine shoe department that contained a magic box.

Nowadays we are served by younger, inexperienced shoe sales-men who don't know a sole from a heel; they are putting themselves through college and looking forward to a grander future than sell-ing shoes. But not Monsieur Malette. He was an elderly, impeccably clad, dignified, white-haired lifetime Eaton's man and a world-ranking orthopaedic footwear specialist. He didn't have a job; he had a career and he knew every stitch of every shoe he sold. He greeted Ma and me as befits an honoured guest of many years' acquaintance and ushered us to leather seats while exclaiming at how I'd grown. Producing a sliding metal tray, he measured the axes of my rapidly expanding feet with allowance for the thick wool socks with darned heels that we wore year round. As I was shod with a series of trial footwear I could insert my feet into his magic box and watch my toe bones wiggle within each of the shoes I was trying on. We later discovered that the device emitted X-rays whose radiation equalled the Chernobyl meltdown.

To Ma, comfort in footwear was secondary, ranking several miles after durability. Cows in those days had far denser and stiffer hides; the thickness of the soles could easily protect the wearer from exploding land mines. They were guaranteed not to bend during the first year of use, and they never, ever wore out.

The excruciating first months of breaking in new shoes were the bane of my young life. I lumbered about like Frankenstein's golem, with arches imprisoned in unyielding sandwiches composed of triple-thickness leather soles; the uppers were uncreased and trimmed, brogue style, not to be confused with a work shoe. Just as my feet were finally assuming the shape of the footwear and the leather was, at last, reluctantly flexing, it was time to return to Monsieur Malette to consult on another pair before my toes fused together.But, before I pass on, I will leave instructions to check, after life is extinct, if my feet glow from Monsieur Malette's magic box.

My Pa

Pa's forebears survived for uncounted generations in Galicia, originally part of the ancient Kingdom of Poland and later a province of the Austria-Hungarian Empire ruled by the Hapsburgs. When surnames were arbitrarily distributed, our clan acquired "Reich" as a patronym. It conveyed no distinction, no advantages, and didn't change their lives as Jews scratching out livelihoods in their tiny *shtetels*. The Great War of 1914-18 brought about the collapse of the Empire. Galicia, inhabited by Polish town dwellers, Ukrainian peasants, and a substantial minority of Jews, became a battleground and its frontiers were re-drawn as the fortunes of war dictated. Between the World Wars, it was incorporated into Poland, then occupied by the Germans as part of the Greater Reich and with their defeat, became part of the USSR. Now Galicia exists within an independent Ukraine.

Rulers succeeded each other, but Jews, the Chosen People, did not lose their standing as victims. No matter who was in power,

My grandparents. Above, Shulem Reich and Leah (Hartman) Reich, whom
I never met, lived in Terszow, Galicia, now a province of the Ukraine. Below,
Avrum Leib Ivry , who arrived in Montreal from Lithuania in 1910, and Chaya
Tzipporah (Yavorovitz) Ivry, who joined him in 1923 with Ma.

they were always identified with the opposition and punished accordingly. The more fortunate, energetic, or enterprising scattered across the earth, enriching many countries.

* * *

My Pa was one of six Reich children of a family living in that embattled area. The three youngest, Mordkhe, Hirsch, and Nute (Marcus, Harry, and Nathan), seeing no future amidst their hereditary persecutors, bade farewell to their parents, two sisters, a brother, and their families. They became Canadians, safe from the fate that awaited those left behind.

Pa, like many others, had arrived in Montreal with no marketable skills, no English and less French, but with a good commercial sense, ambition and an eagerness to work. And work was at hand: he mastered the art of scrubbing restaurant floors. But not for long; he moved on to Nirenberg Travel, an agency that exploited his command of Eastern European languages. His salary rose to the princely sum of forty dollars weekly.

In his spare time, Pa sought out items he considered saleable and peddled them to small retail shops. Eventually he and his brother, Marcus, rented space to stockpile merchandise and Reich Brothers Limited was launched. To us it was known as The Store.

Pa's work took all of his time and energy. When not in The Store, he napped, a skill he perfected and passed on to his sons. On festive occasions, wealthy ladies donned their furs, a sure barometer of success in the "new world." Their knowledge of wildlife was limited to the relative merits and costs of these garments: *poshalem* (*Persian lamb*), or seal, or beaver, or mink. Fancier *grandes dames* sported red fox stoles whose tiny heads with pointy, sharp teeth bounced around their wearers' shoulders as they tottered on high heels while practicing to be ladies.

Pa had no interest in fashion, the arts, music, or anything noncommercial. He never pretended otherwise. I never saw him read a book. Although he had a good sense of the ridiculous, I never heard him tell a joke. He didn't attend concerts, lectures, or athletic events. He didn't play cards or golf; he was not a joiner or a volunteer. He

Harry (my Pa),
Nathan, and Marcus
Reich in 1919 before
they left for Montreal.

unobtrusively enjoyed his life; shy and self-effacing, he didn't
indulge in repartee and seldom spoke to more than one person—
well, maybe two—at a time. Although quiet himself, he admired
liveliness in others. He detested surprises, uncertainties. He lusted
for nothing and was thankful for what he had. A relatively early
immigrant to Montreal and a generous contributor to community
charities, he never served on a committee and refused every office.
He neither needed nor sought praise, recognition, honours, or
awards. He was a gentle man with simple wants. Kind. Undemons-
trative. There was no envy in him, no bitterness, no malice. He
wished to be left alone, unnoticed; his family, The Store: that was
his world. It may have been narrow, but he knew it well; in it he was
comfortable and safe. He was content.

His politics were simple. His only strong opinion was a detestation of communism, a strong force with many followers during the pre-war depression. He respected the work ethic and had no burning wish to share its rewards with the lazy or incompetent. The hypocrisies that sustained the USSR and its satellites were abhorrent to him: the show trials, persecutions, suppressions, anti-Semitism—all in the name of a better world—were frauds, a gigantic swindle built on unrealizable ideals.

Pa was not silent, but to me he spoke mostly of what he knew: business. He never confided his feelings or explained the "facts of life," but he told how stock markets operated, how goods cleared customs, how The Store financed purchases in March to be sold in December. I valued our talks. He never lectured me, but instructed by examples that carried unmistakeable messages: "David, Mr. X's son sleeps late and never works....or Mr. Y's daughter ordered a steak in a restaurant; it cost a whole dollar, and she never finished it...". Disapproval dripped from him. I knew what he expected of me.

Pa had no time or patience with meandering. He was all business. When not working, he slept. The Store was a hard taskmaster: the hours were long, the anxieties many. My brother and I understood. We never expected Pa to throw us a baseball, to watch us skate, to meet our teachers, to hike with us, to picnic, run along with us and fly a kite, or, God forbid, to ski with us. He never lit a barbecue, or wrestled with us, or passed "quality time" with anyone younger than himself.

★ ★ ★

Ma and Pa started their lives together in a modest rented flat in the Jewish quarter concentrated around the Main, known as St. Lawrence Boulevard among the English and Boulevard St-Laurent among those who spoke French. To accommodate their firstborn, they rented a second-floor apartment at 5202 Park Avenue. It was a commercial street with heavy traffic. Car horns blew a constant refrain and streetcar wheels screeched on rails embedded in cobblestone paving.

Ma and I on our home street,
Park Avenue, Montreal, circa 1930.

In 1930 they crossed the dividing line between the lower and aspiring middle classes into the upscale neighbourhood of Outremont, where they rented half a duplex at 1279 Lajoie Avenue. Within four years they moved up again, to 778 Davaar Avenue. There were now parks nearby and open spaces between buildings. In 1939, they bought their own house—two floors, a basement, and a garage—at 737 Hartland Avenue. On the south side it shared a common wall with another cottage, to the north was a neighbour's tennis court. Its nine-thousand-dollar price reflected the superior status that they had achieved. The Store was thriving; we had a home, even a maid—and we were all healthy. We were now upper-middle class. Gentiles lived on our block, including a Catholic judge across the street and a few Protestant families only a few doors away. We got used to them. We had arrived.

None of this would have happened in the world our parents left behind. Pa's family, along with forty other households that comprised the Jewish enclave in Terszow, followed teachings of the Beltzer rebbe to the letter; few made the leap from orthodoxy to secularism. If accepted into academies of higher learning, Jews would be relocated, obliged to ignore the Shabbat, be tempted by nonkosher food, and exposed to the venal sins of the world. Inevitably, *payes*, *yarmukes*, and beards would disappear and prayers would be neglected. In short, the student would become a *goy*. Pa did not import these beliefs and despite my lapses from the traditional faith, I never became a *goy*. It was too much fun being Jewish.

But a dark cloud hung over us. War threatened and, despite Pa's efforts his family remained stranded in Galicia. The world tottered over an abyss and we could do nothing.

Dealing with God

In my family, the Jewish High Holy Days of Rosh Hashonah (the Jewish New Year), Yom Kippur (Day of Atonement), and the Festival of Pesach (Passover, celebrating the Jewish exodus from Egypt) were taken very seriously. The more Orthodox also celebrated a gamut of holidays marking ancient agricultural seasons, historical massacres, expulsions, redemptions, and rituals accumulated since God franchised them as His representative. On these occasions, Jewish shops shut their doors, Jewish workers left their workbenches, and Jewish students didn't attend classes where they were marked absent by their gentile teachers. Jews, dressed in their finery, strolled along Park Avenue exchanging compliments, expressing best wishes to friends, admiring their offspring, and enjoying freedom from habitual duties. *Bar mitzvah* boys put on their new suits, females 'fixed' their hair, and wealthier ladies displayed their furs.

Attendance at synagogue for the High Holy Days was obligatory: to atone for past sins, commune with the Almighty, catch up on local gossip, discuss business, complain about taxes, or deplore whatever government was in power. No one drove. We walked, and it was a long way along stone-paved sidewalks to the Chevra Kadisha, our synagogue on Hutchison Street. Services were in Hebrew and sermons in Yiddish. Chanting praises to God was heavy work, and their excruciating boredom remains with me to this day.

★ ★ ★

Then there was Pesach.

We Jewish kids of the first Canadian generation knew with certainty by the age of three that thirty-five hundred years ago we had been redeemed from slavery imposed by a wicked Pharaoh. We also knew that, much more recently, our parents had been redeemed from their European ghettoes. We kids were free: free to study where admitted, free to work where accepted, free to stay at hotels or join clubs where tolerated, free to practice our traditions. We were descendants of a Chosen People who smote our tormentors with Ten Plagues and bravely embarked on a forty-year trek through a trackless desert, nourished by God-given manna and guided by His cloud of smoke by day and His pillar of fire by night. Along the way we picked up stone tablets engraved with Ten Commandments that we passed on to an uncaring world. And we had Pesach to prove it.

Pesach was the crowning event of the year, celebrated by ceremonial meals on two successive nights called *seders*. In keeping with tradition, all dishes and cutlery were replaced by equivalent items never used except for previous *seders*. All breads, cakes, biscuits, and a long list of ritually forbidden products were supplanted by those acceptable for the celebration. *Pesachdik* foods (approved for consumption on Pesach) were prepared, enough to feed the hordes of Hebrews who had fled the Pharaoh. Boxes of matzo arrived, bottles of sweet wine were stocked, sinus-clearing horseradish was grated and sealed, chickens were roasted, briskets simmered, and their juices thickened into gravies that in turn thickened the blood. Yeast-free cakes and cookies were baked to accompany hot tea. The stage was set. The entire family attended.

As usual, the seder was led by *der Onkle*, Harry Sessenwein. As he was my maternal grandfather's brother, his name had been Ivry and I never clearly understood the reason for the change. He had arrived in Canada around 1905, motivated by a sincere desire to avoid service in the Tsar's armies, an occupation with little future for a Jewish boy. As far as our family was concerned, he was virtually a Father of Confederation.

Der Onkle settled in Montreal and became a successful jeweller—reputed, in fact, to be worth many thousands of dollars. He never married and, outliving my Boba and Zaida, acquired the status of family patriarch. This was only normal and natural; he was an imposing pear-shaped figure, as impressive as J. P. Morgan, whom he closely resembled. His dress invariably consisted of a dark cut-away jacket over a vest draped with a gold chain across its equator. The chain was anchored by a large circular watch housed in a vest pocket. Telling time was no rapid glance at the wrist—it was a ceremony. *Der Onkle* would carefully extract the glistening timepiece, click open its gold cover to display its crystal, consult the Roman numerals, and pronounce the time.

Der Onkle always wore a gleaming white shirt replete with gold cufflinks. His impeccable striped silk tie sported a sparkling diamond stickpin: large, but not gaudy. Like many men in the Ivry clan, he had no hair; with his florid, jowled features he could have been mistaken for a director of any Canadian bank. That was, of course, impossible in those years for a Sessenwein, unless, by some miracle, the Sessenwein was a certified gentile.

There was, in fact, such a miracle. As I became privy to whispered family secrets, I learned that *der Onkle's* nephew married out of his faith and sired a brood of practicing Catholics who flourish to this day. In Montreal, in the 1920s, these events were rare and privately held. When they happened, they were seldom mentioned and never favourably. In the *shtetls* of Eastern Europe one would as soon wed a Martian as a non-believer. Gentiles in Pa's milieu were almost always illiterate *mujiks*, a generation away from serf ancestors, with an unslakable taste for vodka, a passion for pogroms, and a fondness for vicious dogs. I never met another twig of Sessenwein branch. In those days of de facto segregation, family blood, supposedly thicker than water, vapourized when confronted with a *shiksa* bride and a brood of crucifix-bearing children.

No one could accuse *der Onkle* of being light, frivolous, merry, or humorous. He was solidity, dignity, and gravitas rolled into one. And that was the way he presided over the *seder* feasts.

Eating had to await completion of the prescribed ceremonials. It was mandatory for the youngest participant to ask the Four Questions that would be answered by reading the *Haggadah*. That sacred book recounted the story of the Jews' liberation from an enslaving Pharaoh and exodus from Egypt. Some of the text was

Der onkle, my maternal grandfather's brother, presided over the seder feasts. He was solidity, dignity, and gravitas rolled into one.

sung, some read, all in Hebrew. Each person at the table recited several paragraphs in turn. Crippled by my sketchy religious instruction, I limped through my portions. I was ashamed of my halting, mistake-laden performance, and dreaded displaying my incompetence. I would writhe on my chair as my turn approached, scanning the pages ahead in hope of identifying which paragraphs would befall me, and thereby gain a few moments to untangle the more difficult sentences. It seldom worked.

A sparkling white, embroidered table cloth covered the table; a communal groan would arise when its pristine surface was despoiled by the first of many wine spills that inevitably accompanied filling and re-filling our cups as the service progressed. Our *seder*, although falling short of most demanding traditional practices and far from the strict observances of Pa's youth, suited us well. Lubricated by sweet red wine, family singing was merry and boisterous. Everyone left the table with a contented smile and a loosened belt.

Our *seders* were inextricably linked with the Stanley Cup, a trophy awarded every year to Canada's best hockey team. Our immigrant friends and relatives were supremely uninterested in *goyim* skittering about on ice, chasing a rubber disc and slashing each other with wooden sticks, but we youngsters were all great fans and enthusiastically followed the fortunes of our favourite teams. Pesach coincided with the final playoffs, and usually a crucial game was played on one of the *seder* nights. In pre-television days, games were broadcast on radio. To keep us informed, scouts were regularly sent from the seder table to answer a Fifth Question: "What's the score?" It provoked more interest than the entire *Haggadah* that had been the same for over three thousand years and contained no surprises. No one objected; our religious obligations were flexible. And who knew? Perhaps the Almighty might be interested in the fate of the Montreal Maroons or the Canadiens.

And that was Pesach.

★ ★ ★

Der Onkle also came to dinner every Sunday noon at our home, where Ma assembled a meal that could have fed the Russian regiment that his emigration saved him from. We gathered around the table supported by massive round legs milled from walnut tree trunks. Those sturdy legs were needed to support the meal Ma had prepared: bowls of chicken soup with *knaidlach* (little dumplings), platters of roast brisket, dismembered fowl with their gravy boats, side dishes of tzimis (baked mashed potatoes or carrots,) and potato *latkes* (pancakes). Food at these dinners was a renewable resource: the more we ate, the more there was. The meal ended in a clatter of teacups, as honey cake and sponge cake had to be washed down.

My father and *der Onkle* then headed for sofas in the living room, where they were asleep within seconds. Ma and her sister treated the family crockery to a sink frothing with kosher soap, never dreaming of dishwashers or even rubber gloves.

My brother and I divided up the Sunday comics and avidly followed the adventures and mishaps of *Terry and the Pirates*, *Dick Tracy*, *Little Orphan Annie*, *Mutt and Jeff*, *L'il Abner*, *Maggie and Jiggs*, *Major Hoople*, *Katzenjammer Kids*, and many other friends we invited into our home on weekends. On those afternoons we were intimidated into perfect silence while *der Onkle shloft* (the Uncle sleeps). Sleep was holy. I understood that Pa worked from before we awoke each morning until after we finished our supper, six days a week, coming home somewhat earlier on Saturday. *Shabbat* (the Jewish Sabbath) was important, but business, in our family, was business.

The living room where Pa and *der Onkle* napped was, typically, not for living, and certainly not for kids. The room displayed family treasures reflecting growing success in the "new world" and included a deep-piled, richly coloured wool carpet from some exotic Eastern potentate, undoubtedly knotted by dusky children without our advantages. The carpet was surrounded by sofas and chairs framed with glowing dark wood covered with shiny fabric with raised, convoluted patterns, and by precarious end tables topped with lacy doilies and marble-based lamps sporting silk shades stretched over brass frames. A fireplace dominated one wall; of course, nothing ever burned in it. How could it? It was plaster flanked with fluted wood columns tastefully assembled in classical Greek style. At mid-height between the columns was a mantelpiece carrying framed family photos and a full-width mirror topped by a cornice copied from an Athenian temple. Respectability, dignity and good taste reigned.

The sofas and chairs, too valuable to be exposed to risks stemming from children or from spilled tea, were protected by heavy cloth slipcovers. The oak-and-glass doors to the living room were invariably shut, to be opened only on Saturday nights for guests and on Sunday for post-prandial slumber.

Der Onkle was a constant family fixture for Sunday dinners and *seders* throughout the years of my youth. But, inevitably, he declined, and Parkinson's Disease consumed his vast fortune in those pre-Medicare days. He died, immobilized and made stone-faced by illness, leaving my father his diamond stickpin. *Der Onkle shloft*, but now I don't have to be quiet.

Today I Am a Man

A milestone in the life of every Jewish boy is his *bar mitzvah* celebration. On reaching his thirteenth year he is deemed to be on the brink of manhood. Following the prescribed ritual, his birthday is royally celebrated, gifts are lavished upon him and his accession to his new responsibilities is loudly proclaimed. The next day he's back in seventh grade with thirteen-year-old kids. But he's a man.

I looked forward to my *bar mitzvah* ritual as much as a prisoner awaiting his turn on the rack. I would be required to stand on a raised platform in the sparkling, new Adath Israel synagogue, face our entire congregation and chant a portion from the Torah that had to be painstakingly learned letter by letter and note by note. Ma engaged a private teacher for this impossible task: Mr. Brenman was a gentle soul, a sincere pedagogue who did his best to inculcate me with the mysteries of the Hebrew alphabet and the multi-shaped fly specks that passed for vowels for reading and notes for chanting.

Therein lay the problem: I couldn't sing. Not one note. I was a pure *flatto profundo*. Ma's side of the family was musical: she played the fiddle, one of her brothers, Harold, was a professional violinist, and another, Sidney, was a self-taught pianist. But Pa's side of the family was tone deaf. Though the portion of the Torah that I was to chant was mercifully short, it had to be sung from beginning to end. I tried to learn the notes. God knows I tried; He must have suffered if He listened, but He had created me, vocal chords and ear included. Months passed. I grew desperate and my teacher more so. A Ukrainian housekeeper cleaned our home; she was accompanied by her young son. From the other side of the door, the eavesdropping *shaigetz* quickly learned the melody and sang it beautifully. I would gladly have paid him to substitute for me, but he was blond, blue-eyed, and slim; my hair was dark, my eyes brown and I was chubby; someone might have noticed.

I was one of the first lads bar-mitzvahed in that synagogue. My rendition of the holy words was even worse than anticipated. Fortunately, the congregation was forgiving and life went on, but my surviving contemporaries still recall the event and remind me of the debacle. I never sang again. But then, I had never sung before.

The Lighter Side

Socializing was Ma's domain. She had a coterie of like-minded Russian friends, devotees of Slavic poems, plays, novels, and history. On Saturday nights, the group would congregate in one house or another for *kultur abend* (cultural evening); our house was especially favoured. Pa had nothing to do with these activities. Poetry, music, and theatre were not for him, but he drank tea, ate cake, and was content to listen, intervening only when politics was at issue.

I still see those visitors clearly. They have long passed into another world, but for decades they joyfully pushed their way into our home, hugged and greeted each other in an exuberant Babel of languages, and arranged themselves in our living room in happy anticipation of tea, cakes, and culture.

Among them were Morris Goldin, seller of suit linings, and his wife, Sonia, painted and powdered, her tightly curled hair piled atop her head; Mordechai Mendelsohn, the erudite, portly principal of the Adath Israel Hebrew School, whose duties included consulting with gentile principals on basketball rules, although he didn't know a basketball from a matzo ball; Dr. Joe Leavitt, who silently leaned against our imitation fireplace mantel while his wife, Franya, talked for both of them (Joe lived to be a hundred, quiet to the end, but Franya talked herself out much earlier); Sioma Friedman, a dignified, learned typesetter of the *Keneder Odler* (Canadian Eagle), our Yiddish newspaper, who fascinated me with his tales of fleeing Russia to Japan to avoid army service; Shabatai Matthews, a highly successful glove knitter, who would throw his arms around Pa, pound his back, and roar, "Hairie, a dreenk, Hairie," sending my delighted Pa scurrying for a glass of whisky from the lone bottle of Crown Royal enthroned in an ornate, carved-walnut liquor cabinet; Haskell Shiller, a button manufacturer; Sol Magid, proprietor of a modest stationery store; Dr. David Berger, a radiologist. There were many more, all productive, honest folk of good will. They're long gone but vivid memories remain.

At *kultur abend*, literary topics were hotly discussed, poems were read, and music was played. Entertainments were washed down with cakes, tea, and an occasional schnapps. All were immigrants who had arrived with empty pockets and somehow learned to produce buttons, knit gloves, read X-rays, sell suit linings, or import sundries and small ware. Their prosperity, or lack thereof, was immaterial; they were judged on their education, culture, and *menschlachkeit* (honourable behaviour); they earned respect by honesty, generosity, fair dealing, and scholarship. A *mensch*, a man of honour, was esteemed. It was the highest compliment that could be paid. And if they had been unsuccessful in business, Ma would simply say "*Zey habben nisht gahat mazel*" (They were unlucky).

Jennie Reich (Ma) and Sonia Goldin were charter members of the Kultur Abend group, circa 1938.

Sunday evening brought a different mood. The family gathered around the radio to listen to our friends. They didn't know us but we certainly knew them: Jack Benny, the lovable skinflint; Fred Allen, with his nasal voice and bizarre cronies who inhabited Allen's Alley; Edgar Bergen and his wooden dummies, Charlie and Mortimer—their humour was clean, simple, and immediately recognizable. We loved them. Monday night featured the Lux Theatre, a movie transformed into an hour-long radio drama, introduced by the legendary director Cecil B. DeMille and acted out by live stars twinkling in the Hollywood firmament.

We also travelled. True, we never went far in those days; it was too risky. Cars, as balky as mules, had to be cranked to life; they negotiated narrow, winding, bumpy roads, and were coaxed up hills while their drivers anxiously waited for radiators to overheat or tires to burst. Driving was a serious business and it was a rare driver who could report a trouble-free jaunt to the hilly countryside north of Montreal, better known to Ma and Pa as "the Muntins."

In winter, vehicles were stored in garages on blocks, while ploughs, many of them horse-drawn, lined the sides of streets with snow banks so high that we could cross only through paths shovelled at intersections. Streetcar tracks became deep furrows, trapping unwary or inexperienced motorists. When Pa visited customers and delivered parcels by car, he explained to me the mysteries of shifting gears and how to play the brake and clutch like organ pedals. Driving was a chore, not a pleasure.

Our infrequent family outings consisted of Sunday afternoon drives to Cartierville. The thinly inhabited farmland had several major attractions: the Orange Julep, a house-sized sphere from which young ladies in short skirts carried trays of drinks to be affixed to car windows; Piazza Tomasso, where we learned about pasta and pizza; Miss Montreal, a converted tram car in which hot dogs were sold to unsuspecting families not advised by their Mas of the fatal consequences of eating unknown meats. Hamburgers were, of course, out of the question; they were ground from unidentifiable carcasses of dubious origin. I was a teenager before I risked one.

The biggest attraction was Cartierville Airport. In the 1930s, airplanes were rare and when one flew by, activities ceased while we craned our necks at the novel sight. At the airport we crowded around the fence that separated us from the runway and watched daredevils who paid five dollars to invite premature death on a fifteen-minute flight in a shaky, propeller-driven biplane. The waiting line was long and it never included us.

Another rare treat was a visit to Ben's Delicatessen. It is universally known that authentic smoked meat briskets were, and are, produced only in Montreal and exported to uncivilized regions such as Toronto, Los Angeles, and other centres that benefit from Jews who had flown their native Quebec. Smoked meat sandwiches consist of layers of sliced meat thickly stacked between pieces of rye bread slathered with mustard and spiced with *speck*, a lethal delicacy of peppered 100 percent fat. Those inured to serious eating order them with sour pickles or tomatoes and a black-cherry soft drink; it has no equal in the gourmet world.

Entertainment and leisure were never far from home, and were found mostly in hotels, at adult camps, or in quiet, modest resorts in the "Muntins." A favourite was Westerman's Hotel in La Macaza, about a hundred miles north of the city. There, thirteen dollars a week provided a comfortable bed, more-than-ample kosher meals, and access to lush forests thickly inhabited by black flies in early summer and mosquitoes for the rest of the season. There were plenty of chairs and a garden swing large enough for two readers of Yiddish newspapers. Athletically inclined guests played chess, or floated in the river, or tossed horseshoes. Excitement consisted of arguments between members of opposing political parties or Zionist factions; anyone could ignite a room of otherwise placid Jews by mentioning communism or fascism. After two weeks, every-one returned home with enough fresh air, sunshine, and insect bites to last another year.

YOU COULD LOSE AN EYE

Ma's Guide to Survival

For a Jewish kid in the 1920s and 1930s, growing up in Montreal was an ongoing struggle to preserve life, limb, and eyesight. Risks did not stem from vodka-crazed goyim rampaging through the shtetl streets from which our parents had fled; they arose from everyday, quiet life in our adopted Canada.

No Jewish mother worth her kosher salt did not, weekly, daily, or even hourly, remind her kinder of ocular dangers. "You could lose an eye" was her constant reaction to risky activities: these included hockey, skiing, and any freely swinging objects, such as the chestnuts that we gathered from sidewalks, tethered to strings, and swung at each other. These and several thousand other activities documented by our vigilant parents ensured a career with a white cane and tin cup.

Of course, the threat to eyesight was only the tip of an iceberg. Approaching any animal with more legs than we had was dangerous, especially if it had teeth, hooves, or claws. Dogs, identified with vicious peasants from the old country, were particularly well known to be antagonistic to Jews. Drinking cold water when overheated was a leading cause of death, comparable to standing in drafts of any temperature. Other shortcuts to the hereafter included swimming within two hours of eating, or inviting sunstroke by remaining bareheaded in the hot sun, or pneumonia by being hatless in cold weather. Ground meat of unknown ancestry served in a restaurant was universally recognized as a poisonous collection of putrid and otherwise unsalable animal parts, of interest only to non-observant Jews and other collectors of intestinal worms and parasites.

Life was a narrow path, overgrown with scarlet fever, diphtheria, and blood poisoning. Quarantine notices warning of contagious plagues were regularly posted on front doors. Our only antibiotics were chicken soup and hot tea with honey; cut skin was painfully smeared with iodine; gargling with saltwater cured sore throats, and inhaling it through the nostrils cleared sinuses. "You could lose an eye" was drummed into us. I developed a native caution well suited to my natural conservative persona: risk was not on my agenda. It was risky enough to be alive.

Surviving Fun

Fun, of course, was the one all-encompassing activity to be avoided by the entire family, not because it was intrinsically dirty, but because it interfered with studies, work, and whatever needed doing to care, feed, instruct, or comfort the family and ensure its future. Fun, to a Jewish parent, was a waste of precious time. I didn't utter the word in Ma's presence as it prompted immediate and adverse reaction, along with snide comments on my last report card.

Our official entertainment menu was skimpy. Television had not been conceived, and movies were forbidden to those younger than sixteen. But we had radio, and my brother and I thrilled to the daily adventures of Little Orphan Annie, parcelled out in fifteen-minute packages by Ovaltine, whose tinned cocoa was guzzled by its young audience. Thirst was stimulated by the prospect of exchanging a label from a tin for a ring that decoded secret messages. And radio posed no ocular threat.

I was an early devotee of wood blocks. They magically became houses, fire stations, skyscrapers or whatever I imagined. They also had letters and numbers carved on each of their six surfaces that, when properly aligned, could actually spell words. I had discovered the Rosetta stone to literacy.

From wood blocks I graduated to Erector and Meccano sets, whose miniature steel pieces could be joined by bolts and nuts into countless combinations. I couldn't know in those early days that these toys nudged me toward my future career as an architect. One day Pa surprised me with me a printing press, with lead type and

My brother Lionel and
I were constantly enjoined
to avoid having fun, circa 1937.

inky rollers; I became a writer, printer and publisher, all rolled into
one.

* * *

Every afternoon when I got home from school Ma would interro-
gate me about my day while injecting me with milk and chocolate
cake to avert starvation and stave off anorexia. I was then free until
sundown or supper, whichever came sooner. Mostly I cavorted with
our gang on the streets. It was safe; we were too poor to be kid-
napped and child molesters were unknown. We played every possible type of outdoor game. There was always Hide and Seek.
Old-timers will recall Stando, in which runners, frozen in their
tracks upon a signal, were pelted with a ball; Against the Wall, in
which we flung our bodies on each other, forming human mounds;
American Baseball, played by throwing a tennis ball against stairs
and running around improvised bases, usually on neighbours'
lawns; touch football, for which we used a tennis ball; and countless variations of contests involving keys or marbles. Treasure hunts
with obscure clues were fun. Every street had its own traditional
games; they now exist only in fading memories. Kids don't play on
streets any more; they're too busy being chauffeured from lesson

to lesson and from practice to practice—they don't know how to waste their time growing up.

As we grew older, organized sport took root. Despite Ma's incessant warnings, we played ice hockey on nearby rinks and baseball where space permitted. When rinks were unavailable, we enjoyed street hockey with pucks improvised from frozen turds furnished gratis by the horses that pulled delivery wagons. In those depression days, little money was wasted on equipment. Shin guards were school scribblers worn under wool stockings; there were no face masks, no shoulder guards, or helmets; only thick winter clothing and God's compassion for children stood between us and extinction. Because I was a poor skater, I was usually picked to be the goalie. Fortunately, my quick reflexes enabled me to avoid flying pucks, sparing Ma from any worries about a possible hockey career.

Winters usually arrived in November. They were colder then, and snowier. As fast as flakes fell they were ploughed into continuous mountain ranges lining each side of the street. At intersections, workers shovelled passages for pedestrians. Eventually, the mountains were cleared by ferocious machines: trucks with ominous rotating grinders flung snow over the sidewalks and onto our front yards. On main streets the snow was blown into trucks and carted away for disposal. Of course, deep accumulations promoted construction of snow forts, where we lay hidden, armed with snowballs, waiting in chilled silence to ambush unsuspecting passers-by. The forts were often connected by tunnels, that, Ma feared, would collapse, smothering their occupants. And, if the tunnels ran under snow banks along the street, a juggernaut with whirling blades operated by a heedless driver might mince their concealed occupants into hamburger. We heard these predictions several times daily.

An adjacent park had a tower, with an open upper level reaching at least two storeys into the sky. When temperatures were low enough, a steep ramp carrying two adjoining ice-coated lanes was attached to the upper level, forming twin bobsled runs that continued downward through the length of the park and ended in a snow bank. I would pull my toboggan to the upper level, prostrate myself on its cushioned surface, and fly down the run at a hundred miles an hour, maybe more. The ice would blur past, inches from my head, as I clung desperately to the toboggan until it swept up the finishing snow bank. I would triumphantly brush off the snow and, with great excitement, return for another trip. And yet another. It was glorious. Ma never knew.

Summertime also held great treats. A full-size baseball diamond existed in Rockland Park that separated railroad tracks from residential areas. Every Sunday, teams made up of city workers played scheduled softball games. Softball is more intimate than its senior cousin, professional hardball: the bases are closer together; the ball is larger and is delivered underhand. Except for the catcher and first basemen, no one wore mitts; city workers' hands, thickly calloused by shovelling horse droppings and mountains of snow, were far tougher than leather. We crowded onto wooden bleachers four rows high; the pitcher windmilled the ball toward home plate, and the game was on. We watched in awe only a few feet from the intense action and added our voices to the shouts of base runners flinging themselves around the diamond.

What activities were permissible? Clearly, no one was ever bitten by a book, or attacked by a multiplication table, or pecked by a roasted chicken, or kicked by a cow after it had been slaughtered, cut up, sold to Ma, and served as brisket, chopped liver, or rib steak. Life was simpler if you ate three hearty meals daily, with snacks as required to avoid eating on an empty stomach.

I wouldn't be honest if I claimed that I was unaffected by this aspect of my upbringing. It accorded with my temperament and my physical limitations. While my friends were happily flying down hills on their skis, or roller skating in traffic, or playing with bows and arrows, or donning scuba-diving gear, or risking dismemberment or death in a hundred ways, I was able to convince myself that caution was a cardinal virtue. I replaced these suicidal urges with more sedentary pastimes. I'll never know what I missed. But I still have both eyes.

We still have both eyes, even after holidays with our parents in the "Muntins," circa 1934.

Drawing the Curtain

Were we happy? The question never occured to us. Ma and Pa, weighed down with ancestral angst and day-to-day duties, didn't waste time with philosophical concepts; they did what was needed to better our lives and ensure our futures. They were content. I never heard: "We can't afford this or that"; we had enough; no more was needed.

But not far below the surface lurked demons common to those who had emigrated, left families behind, and found success in new surroundings. Insecurity and anxiety bred from generations of oppression did not disappear with abundance and peaceful neighbours; security was sought by fostering tightly knit nuclear families. Death of a member was therefore very deeply felt.

Both Ma's parents had passed away before I was three years old and her sister, Leah, died in 1933, shortly after giving birth of Maier. Marcus, Pa's brother and Miriam's husband, had always been a deeply worried man. It was said that when he was in the front office of The Store, he agonized over the state of the shipping room and when he was in the shipping room the front office was at risk. In truth there was no place where he didn't invent or exaggerate disasters. At least one of his worries were real: he died in 1950 of bone cancer, aged only 53. He left two children, Harriet (Susi) and Lawrence. Susi had a successful career in medical research; Lawrence graduated from law school before suffering the common fate of many other relatives, being ingested into The Store. Worse was to come.

In 1940, Ma began to have difficulty walking. Examination revealed a small growth between her vertebrae compressing the spinal cord. Neurological surgery of that era was primitive and the ensuing operation removed part of the nerve along with the growth. Her recovery was incomplete and she needed another operation. By 1950, she was bedridden. We converted the dining room into a bedroom and the den into a bathroom large enough for wheelchair access. Due to her immobility, Ma developed bedsores that penetrated to her bones. She spent a year in the Montreal General Hospital; for a much longer time she needed constant attention to disinfect and bandage her lesions. They healed with agonizing slowness. Nurses came and went, but her youngest sister, Miriam constantly tended her since her husband's death.

While Ma sickened, Pa aged in good health. He could crack prune pits with his teeth—an exercise whose only utility was to demonstrate his robust molars. Every year, he went on a cruise, returning with ornate ships' menus, beautifully printed documents that awed us with their vast variety of exotic dishes, none of which we recognized. Pa remained hale, hearty, and shy, seldom sharing innermost feelings, although his inborn anxiety always remained with him. He gradually left management of The Store in the hands of his nephews and my brother. His days in the office were interspersed with visits to his stockbroker, naps on the couch in his office that grew in frequency and duration, and swimming interminable laps in the pool that occupied the lower reaches of the Young Men's Hebrew Association. His life remained as uneventful, tranquil, and unobtrusive as he wished.

Although he never understood exactly what I did, Pa was quietly proud of me. I never thought to invite him to my office or to devote more time to him before he was struck by our family disease, *freg nisht*, which settled into his liver and killed him within a few months

I am the child of these parents, circa 1946.

in 1970. It was my loss—and his. He died as quietly as he had lived. I'm certain that the Almighty did not hear him tiptoe into Paradise.

Ma's disabilities progressed. Miriam attended her every day, supervising nurses, washing and changing dressings, keeping her clean and fresh. Fortunately she lived only minutes away. She devoted herself entirely to raising her own children and keeping Ma alive. And so it was for thirty-two years.

My sick Ma survived my healthy Pa by two years. She never complained, never bemoaned her fate as her bodily systems deteriorated. She spent her last years in Maimonides Hospital, the last stopping place for the chronically ill. She wrote Yiddish poetry, assembled ceramics onto trays with failing hands, and died in 1972 in full possession of her formidable faculties, imperious to the last.

Pre-occupied with my own life, I never appreciated how Miriam had sacrificed her own. In 1979 she sold her home and lives alone in a comfortable downtown condominium. At the dawn of her hundredth year, with her children and grandchildren living in other cities and friends having long pre-deceased her, she keeps her active mind occupied playing bridge with a fine circle of Québécoise ladies of her vintage, contentedly winning as much as a dollar a session. Miriam contributed family information from her early days and this book owes much to her. Her long life, much of it taken with unselfish service to others, deserves much more than can be repaid.

★ ★ ★

Through the years, Miriam was in close contact with her contemporary, cousin Billie Ivry. This remarkable lady passed away in 2008, at least one hundred and two venerable years of age. My grandfather's brother, Israel Isaac Ivry, was blessed with eight sons and two daughters. They came from Lithuania to the United States and settled in New York. The youngest, Esther, Americanized into Billie, made her American debut in 1906 as a babe in arms. Two siblings died young, but the rest lived long and productive lives; her numerous nieces and nephews are now in their fifth generation.

Despite Billie's good looks, bright personality, acute intelligence, and sparkling humour, she never married. Starting with a degree from Hunter College, she taught school before becoming the personal secretary to the Chairman of United Stores. Her executive experience over more than thirty years launched her into a highly successful career as a stockbroker. A generous donor, she celebrated her hundredth birthday with a munificent gift to Yeshiva University, highlighting the banquet in her honour with a well-received speech.

I loved Billie. My trips to New York are few, but memorable. My first was as a teenager. Billie greeted me at Grand Central Station, accompanied by Sam, an aspiring suitor who would have died for her. Luckily he didn't have to—he was there to carry my luggage. He would have carried the Empire State Building if only she'd marry him. She never did. He died a disappointed bachelor and was succeeded by another personable but equally unsuccessful candidate. And another. Billie's beaus eventually passed away, but she carried on her independent life in her modest New York apartment on 10th Street. Her eyesight failed and centenary ailments intruded, but her voice on the telephone never changed; it was as peppy as ever until she peacefully departed.

I was convinced that somewhere in an attic her portrait was aging, but, like Dorian Gray, she was untouched by time up to the end.

Bea, her sister, had married Abe Ernst, a successful zipper manufacturer. Abe was a forceful, Type A personality. He twitched with energy. Bea did not adjust well to twitch-level stress and she enjoyed a series of nervous breakdowns that she treated assiduously at spas. Predictably, Abe had a fatal stroke and Bea re-married. Abe's successor, Phil, was closer to Type Z and caused no nervous breakdowns; I remember them wintering contentedly in Florida. The new husband was a dandy; he never passed a mirror without smoothing his hair, stroking his moustache, or straightening his tie. We called him Fancy Phil.

One of Billie's brothers married my Aunt Rose, the widow of Sol, of the renowned Moon Brothers. Rose always referred to him as *Mymorris*. Although he was forgetful, he talked more than her first husband ever did and they lived to venerable ages. For me, Billie was untouched by time, moving purposefully through life trailed by a succession of faithful but disappointed lovers. I hope that, as she reposes in Paradise, the Master *Shadchan*, who matched Eve and Adam, will find someone to suit my Billie.

★ ★ ★

I am a child of these parents. From Ma, I inherited a romantic streak, an abiding love for literature and history, and whatever artistic ability I have. From Pa, I gained business sense, a strong need for independence leavened by caution and a heavy dose of anxiety. Another legacy was Pa's complete lack of musicality, a distinguishing feature of the Reich clan. If I ascend into heaven, I'll never master a harp, even if the Almighty gives me lessons; there are limits to His miracles.

Pa had a gift for calligraphy that I admired and copied. Eventually, I could faultlessly replicate his script. It was excellent training for my architectural career and remains useful: it impresses my grandchildren.

My wit and my disinclination to manual labour, I learned later, came from Pa's father, Shulem, whom I never saw, met, or spoke to. I inherited my desire for learning, my intellectual curiosity, and my striving to chart my own course from Pa's younger brother, Nathan. I sprang from a good family and my rich life is a tribute to them. To my great regret, it's too late to tell them now. Perhaps I'll be able to in *yenner velt*. Ma bequeathed me a rich legacy; I write today from seeds that she planted. Unforgivably, I was too immersed in my career, my family, and my concerns to recognize what I owed her. I always regarded her as a battleship sailing majestically on a course of her choice, indomitable and unswerving, not needing attention or affection. I bitterly regret those lost years; we could have unlocked so much in each other.

THE STORE

The Store is Born

Pa arrived in Canada carrying only his dream. He and his older brother, Marcus, established a business that they called, with sparkling originality, Reich Brothers Limited. We knew it as The Store. It kept our extended family alive and in growing comfort for over three-quarters of a century. The Store is now only a memory, but my existence, and that of most of our *mishpocha*, was inextricably bound up within its walls.

When Pa arrived, he spoke neither English nor French and wasn't hampered by higher education. In his native Terszow, a village of forty Jewish households nestling in the Carpathian Mountains, his family was supported by a small farm and by equally small enterprises that traded in tobacco, liquor, and lumber. This was his business training; it was enough. The world's great commercial centres were not threatened.

Harry and Marcus's first joint venture was in face cream, but the formula was faulty. Chemistry had not been on the curriculum of the Terszow *cheder* that they had attended. The business failed, but another idea caught fire.

Pa had, in his spare time, imported samples that he hoped would sell, and the brothers opened a small shop to distribute them to retail stores. When asked to describe his merchandise, Pa would say he sold anything that started with the letter A: A pencil, A toy, A game, A hairpin . . . These items, typically available in what were then called five-and-dime stores, were known to the trade as sundries, smallware, or novelties. To us, they were bread and butter.

The Store was first located on the Main, a central street lined with small shops almost universally owned by Jews wriggling upstream in the "new world." We never knew it by its proper name, Boulevard St-Laurent; nor did anyone else.

The Store Grows

Business flourished. Increasing numbers of wood crates arrived from exotic lands and their contents were distributed to retail stores at wholesale prices. Sales grew. The staff increased, and in 1939 The Store moved to larger quarters at 70 rue de Brésoles in the grungy, bustling waterfront district of Vieux Montréal. The structure, originally used to store gunpowder, was well over a century old and solidly built of heavy timber supported on limestone-clad brick walls that had never known insulation. Steam pipes from a prehistoric boiler hissed ominously, feeding coils too hot to touch. Bare bulbs dangled from ancient wires hooked over porcelain knobs. Windows of single glass filmed by a hundred and fifty years of soot-laden air glowed dimly in the bright sun. Nothing had changed, except that gunpowder had been replaced by Pa's imports from exotic lands. I knew them from stamps mailed from fabled countries such as Japan, China, and Hong Kong. For the next forty years, the seventy thousand square feet of rented warehouse, spread over seven floors, were filled with "A" merchandise.

The Store was situated conveniently close to docks where goods arriving by sea could be quickly cleared by customs and delivered to our shipping room. The building's proximity to the harbour ensured a thriving population of large rats that no cat would dare approach. Despite the rodents, Reich Brothers became Montreal's largest wholesale smallware importer.

By day, the harbour area was a beehive of noisy truck traffic. The narrow streets, squeezed between large, grimy warehouses, were clogged with trucks carrying cargo to and from the docks, trailing noxious fumes while angrily blaring horns at each other. By night, the streets were deserted, frequented only by intrepid souls of dubious repute, by drunken sailors, and an occasional derelict.

Reich Brothers Limited became Montreal's largest wholesale smallware importer. Uncle Marcus stands ready for business.

The ground floor of The Store was occupied by offices, a showroom, a shipping room, and a long counter that accommodated customers who sought a few bargain items—mostly peddlers, hole-in-the-wall merchants, and carnival booth operators. These small-time entrepreneurs were charming rascals, living by their wits, poor in everything but fanciful stories. They leaned against the length of that counter like cowboys at a bar, discussing politics, sports, their latest swindles, and the travails of life; it was a *shmoozers'* paradise that my brother Lionel happily joined.

But the firm's profits were derived from large department stores. Substantial orders came by mail, or from buyers deferentially received in the showroom. Sidney wooed important customers. He would have been vice-president of sales had such grandiose titles existed in our family. He was one of many relatives who fulfilled their destinies in The Store. Nepotism fed us all.

In and around the shipping room, cases of imported goods were directed to upper floors where they would be delivered of their cargo and their contents stored on open shelves. Outgoing orders were assembled, wrapped in newspapers, and squeezed into recycled cardboard boxes. The gouged wood floor, littered with carcasses of crates, resounded with crashing nail-pullers, creaking jimmies, and banging hammers. Cases were juggled, stacked, and assembled or deconstructed, but not scrapped; even their bent nails were straightened and reused. Unrestrained pandemonium reigned.

The second floor was lined with shelving from floor to ceiling carrying items displayed in the showroom below. They also accommodated my Uncle Harold, whose former profession as a nightclub violinist predisposed him to daytime slumber. He was known to doze on ladders accessing upper shelves; although amiable and willing, he was not considered executive material.

The top five floors were reserved for crates of merchandise stacked and lined in dimly lit rows, their rough wood boards stencilled with inky hieroglyphics identifying their interred contents, like a ghostly necropolis of an extinct civilization. Crates and cartons were transported horizontally on heavy-duty steel-wheeled hand trucks manhandled by muscular shippers and carried vertically in freight elevators that predated Otis; the pyramids might have been built with them. These were wood platforms enclosed on three sides with deeply scarred boards: the front was open. A crosspiece over the top was hooked to cables that disappeared into an attic. When travelling upward, operators had to keep their body parts well inside the platform to prevent them being trapped by each passing floor. Fortunately, the lifts shuddered upward slowly. Users activated them by pulling thickly corded steel wires that adjoined the platform and ran the full height of the building. A skilled operator could stop the platform close enough to a floor to permit hand trucks to enter or leave. I don't recall any accidental deaths during their years of operation, conclusively proving the existence of a God.

Goods came and went through shipping doors opening on Rue le Royer, a narrow back street that served other warehouses and stores along its constricted length. It was constantly gridlocked as trucks backed against the doors to receive or discharge loads. To

The Reich-Ivry families, circa 1932. L. to r., Aunt Miriam (Ivry) Reich, my Ma Jennie (Ivry) Reich, my Pa Harry Reich, Uncle Nathan Reich, then a student, and Uncle Marcus Reich.

position themselves, drivers engaged in two-dimensional space wars: the air rang with furiously blaring horns, malignant French curses, and threats of extreme bodily harm as they dodged each other by millimetres. This frenetic activity continued into the night until the last truck was emptied or filled.

★ ★ ★

Pa's business talents didn't extend to anything involving construction, repairing or use of any tool. He never fixed anything. He couldn't.

Certain humans are born with a supernatural ability to fix things. These specialists realize immediately what has to be done—and do it—with a hammer, screwdriver, paper clip, chisel, or any one of the mysterious *watchamacallits* they carry in tool boxes. In the course of fixing, they invariably discover they lack the *exact* screw they need.

They happily visit a hardware emporium to engage in a long, mutually enjoyable discussion with a fixer-salesperson, one skilled in recommending any of the countless items in small gray boxes that only he can find on shelves that line dimly lit aisles.

There were no fixers in our family. If we possessed a screwdriver, I never saw it. Or a hammer or a wrench. Any fixing we needed was, in our current vocabulary, *outsourced*. We had two major resources who busied themselves in the service of our extended family. Mister Stock and Mister Gursky. I'm sure they had first names, but I never knew them. They were Misters to everyone.

Mister Stock was an infallible authority on all manners of construction. Today he would be called a carpenter, but he was much more. He wasn't a mere woodworker; he was a master craftsman, a jack-of-all-trades, capable of doing anything with tools. Had I been told he'd built the Taj Mahal, I wouldn't have raised an eyebrow.

He often plied his trade at The Store, seventy-thousand square feet of warehouse divided over seven storeys, each filled ceiling-high with wood shelves constantly being emptied and re-stocked. Hand trucks loaded with boxes rumbled non-stop to and from the shipping room across worn wood floors. In The Store there was always something for Mister Stock to fix or build.

Mister Stock was tall, strong, with a nose befitting a Roman emperor and he was never without his large wood box filled with wondrous tools. I watched, fascinated, as he took out his folding rule and unlimbered its short lengths into a rickety line of connected yellow sticks covered with black markings, held it against the object of his visit, squinted at its hieroglyphics and jotted notes with a pencil he carried behind his ear. He made cryptic calculations, muttered to himself and finally delivered a message describing his intentions and their cost. Within days, wood boards and mouldings appeared and Mister Stock transformed them into useful articles. He had the authority of a high priest. His vestments were sawdust-covered overalls made of pockets sewn together that carried everything he needed—except that one exact screw.

Nothing was ever done without Mister Stock; like the Pope, he was infallible.

Mister Gursky was a plumber: short, squat, stubby, and smeared with grease. He was summoned to minister to leaking pipes or to overflowing or non-flowing toilets. His arrival was invariably announced by clanging tools and metal fittings he carried in a burlap potato sack slung over his shoulder—a lumbering Quasimodo who produced music from his plumbing pipes instead of cathedral bells.

Once on site, he would empty his noisy sack onto the floor, select implements and proceed with occult operations that I now recognize as cutting, threading, soldering, or caulking pipes. Neither I, nor anyone else in the family, understood what he was up to, but when he left, water flowed and toilets functioned. Clever Mister Gursky!

Mister Gursky ultimately retired, sack and all. He was replaced by another, whose name isn't even worthy of mention. He immediately displayed his ineptitude. Water leaked from the ceiling into my Aunt Miriam's living room. The substitute Mister Gursky pontificated: "there's a leaky pipe inside the floor," and he proceeded to demolish a substantial part of the soggy ceiling. There was no pipe. He sent a bill for his services. My Aunt replaced the ceiling and the plumber.

No, there was only one Mister Gursky.

Years later, I became an architect. My urge to build wasn't inherited from Ma or Pa; I later learned that a great-grandfather had built houses in their shtetel in Galicia. His genes had leaped over a couple of generations and I was their happy recipient. To the surprise of Ma and Pa I had, in my own way, become a fixer. I knew the mysteries of construction and could make buildings rise from the ground, brandishing only my pencil and paper.

But I never attained the lofty status of Mister Stock or Mister Gursky. My father often asked my professional opinion on problems in our house or The Store; he listened respectfully but double-checked with real fixers: Mister Stock and Mister Gursky.

After all, I didn't have a wood box laden with tools or a sack bulging with fittings and valves.

★ ★ ★

Thanks to Ma's recruiting capabilities, The Store became a one-family *shtetl*.

Few of our clan escaped its irresistible gravity but, in truth, those were hard days; employment was scarce and salaries low. Employees scurried about, filling orders, tottering under boxes, freezing or sweating in under-heated, uncooled, and unventilated work spaces. They included Henri Courtois, a toothless, brawny Hercules who moved cases like they were Rubik cubes and wrenched them apart with fearsome steel claws. He was called the Judge because he had once been summoned for jury duty. He was ably assisted by Armand Turgeon, his short, muscular adjunct, a very obvious reminder of Quebec's Aboriginal roots. There was Ruben Goldstein, his blond hair but a tragic memory, a frustrated singer with a hairline moustache clinging to his upper lip. His falsetto tenor could be heard, non-stop, through the day as he took and filled orders in song. My tone-deaf Pa and Marcus did not appreciate his talents, and Ruben eventually took them elsewhere. Our shipper, Sheldon Cohen, came as a young lad whose father's dilapidated truck undertook local deliveries. Sheldon grew old in the shipping room and today lives in contented retirement, thanks to sundries and smallware.

This was the high-powered team that operated Reich Brothers Limited until the reins were passed to my brother, Lionel, and to my cousins, Herman and Lawrence.

★ ★ ★

Even I worked summers in The Store. When I was strong enough to help with local deliveries, Pa and I filled our recycled cartons with orders, stuffing gaps with the newspapers we had stockpiled. We sealed the box flaps with gummed paper and tied them with rough hemp cleverly knotted into handles. We loaded them into our car and we were off. I marvelled at two of Pa's skills: his ability to shift the floor-mounted gear stick through invisible pathways in the air and his knack of finding an address in Montreal's maze of streets.

At designated locations we dragged cartons up winding, snow-covered steep stairs or slid them down rain-slicked steep stairs. While driving between customers, we talked. He never spun romantic tales of heroic knights, distraught maidens or royal lovers: he spoke of savings and investments, of the workings of the stock market, of how merchandise was imported and exported. He explained how he borrowed money from the bank to buy his goods and how he paid it back. He told me how important it was to keep commitments, to never break promises. It all seemed very risky, but Pa did it.

After the last package was delivered, Pa and I would find a café. Pa drank tea; I had hot, creamy cocoa and an immense oatmeal cookie—nothing else ever tasted as good. We never felt closer than during the drive home at the end of the day. And we didn't tell Ma about my cocoa or cookie—she would have said it would spoil my appetite. She needn't have worried.

Originally Pa had peddled goods from store to store. As the business expanded, he sat in his office and worried if employees, concealed on seven floors, were working diligently and honestly. He worried about the bank loan, payment from delinquent customers, late arrival of goods. Nothing escaped his anxious attention. Worry was an all-weather, all-season occupation. It could be practiced day or night, sitting, lying, or standing, requiring no apparatus, no special lighting. In fact, darkness was preferable: there were no distractions and the worrier's imagination was richer. Pa was ably abetted in his worrying by Marcus; his brother, being older, agonized even more. If anxiety could be bottled, they could have supplied all of Canada and had plenty left over for export.

The workweek was at least five and a half days. When not working, Pa slept. There was no time for frivolity, long lunches, or hobbies. Cards were out of the question: no one in our family knew an ace from a deuce or a jack from a king. Golf was unheard of: who would take time from business to club a ball at a small hole? And The Store didn't sell golf balls. My brother and I never suffered from what might be perceived as paternal neglect. Ma filled our lives, giving enough for both parents. But I learned to worry, and if there was nothing to worry about, I worried about that. Pa would have been proud of me.

When war came, imports ceased. Industry was geared to serve the armed forces, and few consumer products were made. Reich Brothers required ingenuity to fill its shelves. It printed cards,

My Pa and I in the Laurentians.

improvised tokens, and assembled Bingo sets. It boxed rolling pins, spoons, and plastic dishes into children's pastry sets. It found or created merchandise. In that period of shortages, everything sold.

The Store Expires

The post-war period saw the expansion of large retailers with many outlets. Instant communications with foreign suppliers became available and affordable. Distant lands were only hours away as jet aircraft filled the skies, and Eaton's, Morgan's, Dupuis Frères, and other major emporiums could buy directly from the Far East without the intervention of wholesalers. The customer base dwindled as Reich Brothers was left with smaller customers who were more costly to service and less creditworthy. The trend was inexorable.

To meet challenges of the rapidly changing business environment required bold, innovative changes, even a departure from the traditional wholesale format. It was not to be. Changes and improvements were discussed, but unanimity could not be reached and the business continued more or less as before, powered by its own inertia. Moe Blostein was not given to giddy flights of innovation or adventurous initiatives. No, this was the way business had always been carried out and, thank God, it had been profitable. I knew his mantra: "And I'll tell you something else—leave things as they are."

Modernization was not a word commonly associated with Reich Brothers Limited; the suffix "Limited" described this shortcoming. Taking The Store's inventory took a week of counting by hand and filling forms with multiple carbon copies. Accounting was no more advanced; business planning and projections were nonexistent. Computerization, advances in materials handling, storing and checking, electronic communications, business systems, merchandising—all were lacking or introduced too late. The family ethic postulated unanimous agreement on every decision. After all, families didn't fight. So they continued to agree—or, more accurately, to remain deadlocked. There was no boss, no single arbiter capable of implementing policy. There was only compromise that satisfied no one. If it promoted family unity, it also doomed The Store. There was a time when the business might have been sold, but it was decided that sales figures were too confidential to be disclosed to potential buyers. Somehow, this discouraged them.

After Marcus died, Pa slowly withdrew from active participation. Direction of the business devolved on Herman and Lionel, and eventually Lawrence. Herman was the buyer: he visited Japan, China, and other fantastic lands in search of sundries beginning with "A". Lionel occupied himself with customer relations, mostly at the counter, and Lawrence gradually assumed executive responsibilities. The different personalities brought neither changes to entrenched business strategy nor effective responses to the evolving business environment. Decision-making was as gridlocked as the adjoining streets. But change was forced on The Store.

To everyone's amazement, after some forty years The Store was forced to move: the building had been sold to a developer and reinvented as an upscale condominium. The run-down harbour front had become trendy. This ancient warehouse, rats and all, that had rented for ten cents a square foot, led the tidal wave of gentrification. Its dirt-encrusted timbers were sandblasted to their original grained beauty, the ancient cast-iron connectors were painted a rich black, the eroded wood floors were refinished, and the limestone exterior was washed to an opulent antique elegance. Death-trap elevators were replaced by silent, swift, electronically controlled lifts. Rats, unable to afford the high cost of these improvements, departed.

The constricted, truck-filled thoroughfare at the rear was transformed into a quiet garden and traffic was redirected. The echoes of honking horns, gunned motors, and drivers' curses were forever stilled. It was not to be believed; but it happened.

★ ★ ★

When the lease on the Rue de Brésoles warehouse expired, Reich Brothers Limited bought a smaller but more efficient two-storey building with high ceilings and no rats. Although the premises were new, business habits remained unchanged. The downward trend continued unabated until it could go no lower. The space slowly emptied and its upper floor was rented. Finally, the building and its remaining merchandise were sold.

Reich Brothers Limited sank without a trace. Nothing remains except a few words painted almost a century ago on an old limestone wall. It faces a quiet, secluded garden: the old Rue le Royer. When I close my eyes I hear the honking vans, the cursing drivers, the clattering hand trucks: all dead and gone. The space has been transformed into a magic garden where strollers can reflect on a weathered text: Reich Frères Limitée.

EDUCATION AND ME

How We Got to Where We Were

In the wonderful story *The Wizard of Oz*, a straw man follows a yellow brick road in search of the Wizard, hoping to acquire a brain. At the end of his journey, he discovers that the Wizard is a fraud, incapable of miracles, but wise in the ways of the world. Instead of a brain, he gives the straw man a diploma that will serve him equally well, if not better. Our parents never doubted that we had brains, but they desperately coveted those diplomas. Aware of their shortcomings as aliens to English language and culture, immigrants realized that keys to doors labelled "success" were produced in schools. Businesses could be confiscated, houses burned, possessions stolen, and entire populations deported, but knowledge—a profession—was enduring. Needless to say, we never questioned this article of faith. We were ready for the education system, but the system was hardly ready for us.

In the early 1930s, my moderately successful parents crossed the boundary from Montreal into Outremont, where my new address and ancient Judaic religion put me under the jurisdiction of the Outremont Protestant School Board. Despite the preponderance of Jewish students in the jurisdiction, there were no Jewish teachers; they simply were not hired. We were taught by trim, accentless WASPs, defenders of the faith and flag-bearers of the British Empire. They were familiar with mothers and fathers, but not with Mas and Pas who were too shy to expose their immigrant singsong accents and English illiteracy to the correctness of native Canadians, who spoke the King's English perfectly.

With my first lady friend
in pastoral surroundings;
the bashful maiden chose
to remain anonymous,
circa 1932.

The Public School Student

My sixth birthday loomed and I was enrolled in Guy Drummond
Public School. Ma and Pa never visited that institution or any other
school that I attended, but they avidly studied my monthly report
cards. They were aware that a 90 percent grade was better than 80
percent and that 100 percent was better still. They were less comfortably aware that McGill University, the ultimate dispenser of diplomas, was very fussy when it came to accepting applicants,
especially those from the wrong side of the pew, and that our school
records must accordingly sparkle.

Although I was a good student, it wasn't long before my report
cards began to inform Ma and Pa, "David is not living up to his
potential." My teachers could have made a rubber stamp with these
words, as they appeared with unfailing frequency. In fact, I exceeded
my potential. I was a practicing sluggard gifted with a quick tongue,
a strong sense of the ridiculous, an orderly mind, and a power of
expression burnished by omnivorous reading, all of which was

interpreted as dormant genius. My examination marks were not poor, but neither were they exceptional. I was strong in mathematics, literature, and science and especially proficient in language as a result of omnivorous reading and an insatiable hunger for stories instilled in me by Ma's romantic literary tastes. I never heard about pigs in straw houses or girls in red riding hoods, but learned of the savageries of Ivan the Terrible, the cruelties of Empress Catherine, and the adventures of Peter the Great. These instilled a lifelong love affair with literature.

My literary aptitudes were useless in coping with a couple of skills that others readily mastered. I developed, or was born with, a particular antipathy to gym class, an obligatory course that appeared every year on the school curriculum through eleven years of elementary and high school. It would take a compassionate physical education instructor to not give me a failing mark for stumbling around the gym floor and knocking over diabolic equipment that I regarded much as the victims of the Inquisition or the Gestapo viewed their instruments of torture.

When the bell signalled the gym period, I marched with my class down into the bowels of Guy Drummond Public School, and later into similar bowels at Strathcona Academy. The gym doors were flung open to display fiendish contraptions, clearly conceived by anti-Semites to castrate or disembowel in the name of physical education. Particularly threatening was a box assembled from a series of interlocking wood sections, with sloped sides and a cover thinly padded to evoke an aura of security that didn't fool me. Another devilish invention was the pommel horse, consisting of a leather-covered metal frame with two handles on top projecting enough to constitute high risk to my future progeny. These were placed just behind springboards that conjured up a myriad of possible manoeuvres, all of them frightening.

I was required to take a short run, leap onto the springboard, and be catapulted some way onto the box, or over the horse, both of which seemed to grow in height by the minute. The matter was clearly impossible. Either the springboard would surrender and remain bowed under my weight, or the weak flip wouldn't carry my well-nourished carcass to the upper levels of the stratosphere, and my uncoordinated, fearful, and fumbling lunge would fall short of the target. Several huskier students stood about nervously on either side of the apparatus as spotters, responsible for catching my dead weight as I lurched into a misguided trajectory.

There is no need to describe the ensuing debacles. Over an eleven-year span I knocked sections of the box apart and impaled myself on that cursed horse in every way known to klutzes. Even when sympathetic hands hoisted me into place and lined me up for a somersault, I managed to roll sideways to the floor tangled in a heap of hapless spotters.

Ropes were another trial. They hung from the trusses supporting a ceiling five hundred feet in the air and were intended for climbing. I carefully watched the technique of skinnier classmates scrambling to the top like frenetic monkeys. I would take a flying leap at the rope and remain swinging six inches above the floor like the victim of a botched hanging. I was never better than a pendulum. Despite contortions intended to somehow ratchet myself upward, it never happened.

Skiing, of course, was beyond discussion. The idea of strapping a lumberyard to my feet to slide down an icy slope in freezing weather well beyond the reach of hot chicken soup was patently out of the question, all considerations of useless expense aside. We knew for a fact that skiers provided steady income for orthopaedic specialists, all resulting from freak accidents, as if these could be distinguished from the deliberate variety. "Ma, I was standing still, and all of a sudden my leg snapped!" I could hear myself explain. Clearly, without skis it was difficult to have a skiing accident. Pa's memory of the sport in his native Galicia was one of bearded Jews travelling on railways clutching a single ski to benefit from a reduced train fare.

My hopeless gymnastic talents were only matched by a total lack of musicality. I first became aware of this deplorable weakness in an early grade when my music teacher perched on my desk, struck her tuning fork and the class hummed the note. I need go no further; she left my desk as if assailed by a putrid odour. I could never carry a tune, never scale a scale, or distinguish *God Save our Gracious Weasel* from *Pop Goes the Queen*; the Reich gene was too powerful.

* * *

Although Ma was a literary romantic, she was a hard-headed realist in real life. She immediately and instinctively went to the core of the matter or of the person and was merciless in her judgments; she was not clouded by sentiment. For better or worse, I grew to see the world as she did, except that I dealt with folly and hypocrisy through humour; much of the world seemed foolish and hypocritical, motivated by lust for power and by greed. I was not averse to bringing this to the attention of others. Laughter and sarcasm were my tools. These characteristics were interpreted as "potential."

Fierce academic competition, encouraged by our parents, naturally resulted in Jewish monopoly of every school prize except attendance. The few gentile students had the unconquerable advantage of attending an almost empty school on the Holy Days of Yom Kippur and Rosh Hashonah, while their Jewish counterparts, spiffified in new pants and shoes, were dragged off to synagogues and marked "absent" when class attendance was called.

My last year in public school started in September 1939, coinciding with the start of the Second World War. At twelve years of age we became part-time soldiers, dressed in cavalry coats salvaged from the First World War, designed to cover the behind of the wearer's horse. Rifles were made of wood: we shouldered arms, presented arms, trailed arms—and marched. Every week we proudly paraded through Outremont's streets with our toy weapons. Our khaki coats bulged to conform to the rear of an absent stallion and a band drummed and bugled our presence to onlookers who were bemused but not reassured.

The High School Student

The next year, I was in Strathcona Academy, as our high school was pretentiously named. It began inauspiciously. Our beloved principal, on whom we had never laid eyes, died. He lay in state, impeccably dressed, serene and thoughtful, calmly contemplating his funeral procession and interment. The coffin was open, and the entire school body was marched past his corpse. Neither of us was upset and Ma received the news calmly; it had nothing to do with learning.

As the war progressed, we switched from army khaki to air cadet blue. Again, we marched and again we shouldered arms. The schoolyard was large enough to accommodate several platoons directed by sergeants barking rapid-fire commands: "Quick march! By the left! On the right! Left wheel! Squad—halt! Right turn! Quick march . . ." Within minutes, each of us was stepping off—but in a different direction. Somehow, we never got the knack. School courses included meteorology, navigation, and aircraft recognition. We sat in a darkened room and identified the enemy planes that flashed across a screen: "Messerschmitt! Dornier! Stuka! Focke-Wulf! Junkers! Heinkel!" we screamed in excitement. Deterred by our skill in identifying hostile aircraft, not one ever flew over Canada. After four years of high school we could read weather charts and understand forecasts, and had mastered aerial navigation, all without leaving the ground or risking our lives.

But it cannot be denied that the academic level was high. The school was filled largely with first-generation Jewish kids who competed furiously for top honours in Quebec against their counterparts at Baron Byng, the school immortalized by Mordecai Richler. It catered entirely to Jewish children from poorer neighbourhoods. Although only a few blocks removed from middle class Outremont, Baron Byngers were readily distinguished by their accents and by their original grammar by which they are recognized to this day (for example, we *stayed* at hotels; Baron Byngers *stood*).

I cannot neglect this opportunity of mentioning Louise McCuaig. She taught literature and composition to graduating year students. Not only did she reinforce my love for the classics, but was thrillingly supportive of my essays and amateur writings. I never forgot her encouragement and, fifteen years later, repaid her by designing her retirement house in the Maritimes.

High school provided one turning point in my life. In tenth grade, Jacob Siskind, the occupant of the school desk across the aisle from me, asked what I was considering as a career. Jacob was an excellent pianist; he had taken lessons from birth. Ma held him up as a shining example of what a Jewish boy could learn, but I couldn't tell a white piano key from a black one.

I had vaguely considered being a sailor, no doubt fantasizing escape from Ma's omnipresent control and visiting exotic countries whose stamps adorned letters received by The Store from its foreign suppliers. But this was clearly unrealistic. Conventional professions held no allure. I couldn't see myself double-entering figures in account books, or gazing at patients' tonsils as I filled their teeth. Law and medicine were only marginally more exciting. My sole ambition was to not be sucked into The Store. I admitted to Jacob that I had no calling.

Jacob surprised me. Instead of aspiring to a concert stage, he wanted to be an architect. He spoke of design, construction, drawing; these struck a non-musical chord in me. I had never considered architecture. In class I was always doodling fantastic figures or practising calligraphy. As a child, I had been besotted with Erector and Meccano sets. I loved making and remaking anything of wood I could get hands on. Yet architecture had never crossed my mind. Now everything swam into place. That was it. That was what I wanted to do; there was no question.

Jacob became a widely syndicated music critic and then expanded his critiques to include theatre and dance; it was always easier to criticize than to perform. But I was the one who became an architect. It was a happy decision, one that I never for an instant regretted; thank you, Jacob.

Pa wasn't enthusiastic about with my choice; family members were expected to join The Store. But he understood and spared me the guilt of disappointing a parent. In Terszow, there had been no architects. Pa asked for details. I explained that I would design beautiful buildings for clients.

"How will you find customers?" he asked.

I hadn't considered that aspect. "I'll open an office, put a sign on the door, and wait."

"You'll wait? That's not a business! You go to customers and sell them what they need. That's a business."

Pa was right. In the succeeding years I pursued clients. Some thought that I was pushy, but I was only doing what Pa had taught me. Besides, pushiness was natural to me.

The University Student

Completing elementary and high school provided the potential for access to McGill University, at the time a very private, very renowned, and very, very English institution. It was particularly fussy about whom it accepted within its ivy walls. The medical faculty admitted no more than six Jews to a first-year class of one hundred and twenty, and many of the brightest minds in the province were forced to study abroad, study medicine in French schools or excel in other fields. McGill's small architectural school, not burdened with a surfeit of applicants, had no such restrictions. My matriculation marks were high and I was awarded a modest scholarship. In 1944, at sixteen, unworldly, inexperienced, and unsophisticated, I entered McGill University; I immigrated to my "new world."

At university I continued my budding military career as an officer cadet, needing only a failed exam to be flung into the trenches. As an officer in training, I was issued a rifle and uniform with many brass buttons that I was expected to shine before every parade.

Several times a week I panted up University Avenue in full army regalia to the Sir Arthur Currie Gymnasium. Standing at attention, shoulder to shoulder with my brothers-at-arms, I held my head erect with eyes focused forward, daring any enemy to attack. Then, in platoon formation, we marched about responding to arbitrary commands barked by no-nonsense commanders who took these drills seriously. I performed gymnastics with my rifle, fixed and unfixed my bayonet, and assembled and disassembled machine guns. During the summer break I attended military camp. Firing guns was fun; I never hit anybody, or anything.

I completed my first year in the obligatory science program. Even then, I felt the need to examine alternatives and I followed course options that could lead to architecture or engineering or medicine. Medical prerequisites included botany and zoology. I excelled. I could draw whatever I could see through a microscope and was adept at illustrating flora. My professor looked to me as a promising naturalist and was disappointed when I confided my desire to be an architect. But his ambitions for me took root, in a way: my architectural career was largely involved with plants that my botany professor had never envisaged: smelters, mills, concentrators, refineries, and other buildings that sprouted aluminum, paper, cement, steel, oil, and chemicals. Their perfumes were not fragrant, no bees sucked their nectar, and no poets rhapsodized over their metal roofs and concrete walls.

I had no inkling of what awaited me as I entered five years of unrelenting architectural studies relieved only by summers in design offices or on construction sites. I never regretted a single minute of it, instantly taking to drafting, an art that disappeared with the advent of computers forty years later.

At my first interview for a summer job I humbly requested a salary of twelve dollars a week, equal to what sweating in a warehouse earned for me. The architect, Pierre Amos, looked at my work, was impressed by my calligraphy and counter-offered eighteen dollars. I allowed myself to be persuaded. He was not disappointed and neither was I. In those days, drafting was laborious and painstaking; we drew with ink precariously held between adjustable steel blades that formed lines on starched linen. Errors were scratched off with razor blades. My employer, a true gentleman, had great patience with an architectural aspirant.

The next summer, the Canada Mortgage and Housing Corporation hired me as a draftsman in the Ottawa office. I arrived at my new job bursting with ambition, eager to work and exuding diligence and enthusiasm. After being assigned a drawing, I put my head down, started off immediately, and didn't look up from the board as lines flowed from my pen. Soon my supervisor was at my side: "What are you up to? Relax, have a coffee; look at how everyone else is working." I looked. I saw that anyone floating in those stagnant pools of indolence would be washed clean of ambition, initiative, and self-reliance and would spend his life standing around a coffee machine discussing retirement, or the coming weekend, or the shortcomings of his superiors. During that summer, I learned everything I needed to know about government. I never had cause to change my opinion.

The following summer, I worked as a developer's building inspector. Very presentable houses, encased in brick and finished with plaster, sold for seventy-five hundred dollars. Top pay for skilled workers was little more than a dollar an hour in those pre-union days. It was my first experience on a construction site. As the developer's representative, I was referred to as "the spy." My functions included reporting on daily progress, receipt of materials, and distribution of items made scarce by the Korean War.

I was never one of the boys. I dispensed nails one handful at a time, never two. I refused bribes to sign off on materials that hadn't been delivered to our site. I wouldn't certify work that hadn't been performed and reported it if defective. I learned what talent and ingenuity could subtract from a job; it served me well. Best of all, I impressed the neighbours when I was driven home high in the cab of a cement mixer.

The following summers and during Easter, Christmas, and holiday breaks I worked for a local architect. He was short, aggressive and very busy. It was a small office; I was often alone and given responsibilities beyond my experience. I had to learn quickly. Those were hectic days, filled with unrelenting pressure to design, draw, and supervise a flood of projects simultaneously. I had no choice; I designed, drew, and supervised. I quickly learned that clients, contractors, and workers equated dollars with minutes. After a couple of summers, my employer came to depend on me. It was an exciting introduction to the realities of private practice.

As the war sputtered to a close, returning veterans, attracted by free tuition, rushed to enrol in universities. They were impressively older, some by as many as five years, had seen the world, and been targets of enemy bullets and shells. I shared a drafting room with a man who had flown thirty-three missions over Germany, another who had sailed in a corvette escorting convoys, another who commanded artillery—these were heroes. I was a sophomoric tenderfoot who feared to lose an eye. And, for the first time in my life I was mixing with *goyim* who drank beer and talked of riding horses and sailing boats. They intimidated me. They were from another world. But before long we formed lifelong friendships that I treasure.

McGill's Montreal campus could not cope with this crowd of returning servicemen. A new facility was established in nearby Saint-Jean, in a converted military base renamed Dawson College. We slept in barracks and ate in cafeterias. For the first time, I was free of parental supervision and strictures. It was exhilarating.

The following year, our group was back in Montreal, a class of about twenty aspiring architects dedicated to changing the face of the world. The director of the School of Architecture was a newcomer, John Bland. He swept away the cobwebs of traditional classical training and introduced the modern era; a new world was dawning on the ashes of the old. Europe was in ruins; little had been built in America during the war years. We rolled up our sleeves and attacked architecture with a whole new vocabulary, hotly debating the design approaches of Gropius, Lloyd Wright, Corbusier, Van der Rohe, Neimeyer, Aalto, Kahn, and other stars of the revolt against stale, classic design. The revolution involved many elements: art, literature, sculpture were in flux. And we loved it. Five years slipped by in a blinding flash. Days and nights were filled with drawing and designing, constantly striving against our limitations.

I learned to conceive structures in two dimensions on paper and transform them into three-dimensional models. Eventually, as an architect, my designs would become buildings that I could watch grow from foundations to roof. There would be no greater thrill than seeing what I had imagined and depicted in sketches achieve final form. My profession would replicate my childhood. And I would be paid for it!

Realizing that the construction curriculum at McGill was weak, I took correspondence courses in parallel with my studies. Theoretical discussions on the merits of competing architectural styles were important, but construction materials and techniques were not to be ignored: they kept architectural styles from leaking, collapsing, or blowing away. Advancing building technology created new forms that were ultimately accepted. It was all very exciting.

My favourite professor was Watson Balharrie, a senior architect who commuted from Ottawa. His course was construction. He would walk between our drafting tables, glance quickly at our efforts, and, as if by instinct, draw attention to errors, inconsistencies, inappropriate use of materials, and other failings that our inexperienced hands produced. His explanations were simple, clear, and enlightening. I resolved to model myself after him: to produce, simple, clear, rational designs.

We took our work seriously, but ourselves less so. Tex Dawson, a talented entertainer, danced on his drafting table strumming his ukulele to Doug Lee's crooning; we laughed at and with our teachers. Our premises were cleaned by a very fat janitor; we stuffed his overalls, improvised a head, and perched him on our fifth storey window sill while we loudly implored him not to jump. It gathered quite a crowd.

Tex was also a talented artist, and I had acquired a knack for cartooning. Together we produced signs and menus for restaurants. It was a neat sideline and provided pocket money, but our comical cows and hamburgers would never supplant architecture.

Our art teacher was Arthur Lismer. At that time he hadn't achieved renown as a member of Canada's fabled Group of Seven, and his paintings didn't command hundreds of thousands of dollars. I regret that I never kept the quick, sharp sketches with which he illustrated his lectures. To us, he was a quirky, humourous teacher with wispy white hair swirling over his bare skull. He led us during summer sketching school. Tex, brimming with artistic aspirations, had set up his easel beside a bucolic stream and was busily applying his watercolours from a paint box of sixty colours. As he concentrated on meticulously reproducing the scenery, Lismer strolled by. He leisurely plucked a twig from a bush, stirred it into a few paint samples and almost instantly produced a beautiful sketch for Tex's edification. Tex picked up his brushes and paint box, closed the cover, and slung it into the river, resolving to use twigs for his painting. I always admired him for his humour and ability to seize the moment; it never deserted him. After he retired from his architectural practice, Tex successfully returned to art. His lovely seascape of a Nova Scotia fishing harbour adorns my den.

The unquestioned star of our class was Arthur Erickson, destined to be Canada's leading architect. We weren't surprised; his talent was apparent from the start and, although friendly, he occupied his own world. Not for him the comradely light-heartedness of our class with the fumbling efforts of beginners; while we struggled over projects in our common drafting studio, Arthur worked at home, submitting his designs at the last moment. We were in awe. Our class, half of whom were youngsters fresh from high school, the other half returning war veterans only a few years older, had none of Arthur's sophistication, vision, and genius. Our teachers, cognizant of his brilliance, nurtured him.

Gordon Webber, our design professor, was Arthur's mentor; their perceptions left our efforts, as beginners, far behind. Arthur's accomplishments fully justified his promise. In later years I visited Simon Fraser University, Robson Square, the UBC Museum of Anthropology, and other of his achievements. I was never disappointed. Unfortunately, his later career was blighted by an inability to attend to the business side of his profession; genius has its limitations.

I last saw Arthur in 2007; age hadn't ravaged him but he had slowed perceptibly. We discussed several of his current designs. These required sophisticated computer applications for their construction; I asked him how he had adapted to these techniques. "I know nothing about them," he responded. "I can't even turn a computer on." We lunched and had a farewell drink. Two years later he was dead. But his work will always be with us. He was the only genius I've ever known.

Sixteen of us survived our five-year ordeal. Of these, about half disappeared into the great void to the south, the United States; others dispersed across Canada. We who remained in Montreal formed an association without officers, dues, premises, by-laws, or constitution: the RAIUMP-50, short for Rassemblement des architectes inférieurs du Université de McGill—Promotion '50 (Assembly of Inferior Architects of McGill University, Graduating Class 1950). Its mission was to maintain our friendship; it was successful. We lunched together for over fifty years. Three survivors still meet, and we enjoy each other's company as much now as then. Our faces are marked with wrinkles and jowls, but we see each other exactly as we were six decades ago.

Finally we graduated. At convocation, after an inspiring speech, the principal thrust a diploma into my hand. I was an architect. The world awaited me.

My schooling had finished; my education could begin.

I DRAW THE LINE

What This Is All About

The architectural profession holds great attraction for anyone who loves to build, is ready to work like a dog for a modest, uncertain income, is inured against incessant frustration, and doesn't crave appreciation. I wouldn't have changed it for anything; I loved it from the day I first picked up a pencil. I still do.

This Chapter is a travelogue of my fifty-year architectural journey, a route marked by false starts, long uphill stretches, many detours, and excursions into unmapped territories. Thankfully, I was able to disembark from my practice sane, solvent, and full of more memories than can fit into this Memoir.

In 1950 I returned to my former employer as a draftsman, then became his junior partner, and shortly thereafter (as will be described), his former junior partner. The disappointing experience prompted me to launch my own practice in 1952 and after forty years of remarkable and unanticipated adventures I retired as senior partner in a thriving office of about forty hard-working, competent partners, associates and employees. This Section describes some of the challenges that I and my confrères confronted. Now my children will learn what I did after I left the house every morning. It may encourage or warn those considering a similar career.

I had no inkling at the outset that my career would be so demanding and so fulfilling. Although the practice was based in Montreal and concentrated in Quebec, I acquired a diversity of clients who led me over strange and unanticipated paths. In addition to buildings in the United States and across Canada, I designed an airport in Abu Dhabi, a bus terminal in Bolivia, hydroelectric stations in

Malaysia, apartments in Israel, industrial works in Chile, Venezuela, Algeria, and Belize. My airport and the hydroelectric stations appeared on postage stamps of their respective countries; now everyone could spit on my work.

Some projects have appeared on postage stamps.

Several thousand of my houses and apartments now crowd Montreal's suburbs. They are an undistinguished lot, but they enriched many builders during the post-war housing boom. The few that won prizes sold the least. I don't know if this reflects worse on me, or on the competition judges, or on the purchasers.

My homes are in every Cree settlement in northern Quebec. When the La Grande River was dammed to generate electricity, Fort George, on the banks of James Bay, had to be abandoned; I designed all the homes for its replacement, Chisasibi. And if these villages weren't cold enough I was responsible for houses, schools and public buildings for more remote Inuit settlements. These led to housing projects for asbestos workers in Newfoundland and oil workers in Chad. I sweated in Nigeria, froze in Baffinland, and gasped for air in La Paz. I sailed down the Niger River to the ocean and sloshed across its sodden delta accompanied by clouds of famished mosquitoes. What other profession offers such satisfaction? It was FUN. And Ma wasn't there to warn me I could lose an eye.

Not all my conceptions came to fruition. The grandest project I never built was the Parliament Building in the Midwestern State of Nigeria; it was probably not realized because of an acute shortage of Nigerian parliamentarians. Other aborted projects included the prison system for Abu Dhabi and an Inuit village in furthest Baffinland for workers to exploit a mountain of pure iron ore. My client asked me to suggest a name for the village that had an Inuit flavour. I proposed *Oomglick*. When it was discovered that the shipping season wasn't longer than a week, the iron ore was left undisturbed and the town was never built. Had the shipping season been longer, *Oomglick* would have appeared on the map. Just as well: it's the Yiddish word for misfortune, disaster or calamity.

As an architect, I was a rarity: few in our profession knew or cared about designing industrial buildings; they earned few prizes or little recognition. I cared a lot: they presented difficult challenges that demanded considerable research, the owners had few preconceptions concerning their appearance, they involved travel and intimate contact with culturally diverse peoples, and—most of all—they paid well.

My single most important client was the engineering group that grew from Surveyer Nenniger Chenevert, to become known as SNC-Lavalin. Camille Dagenais was the SNC senior partner, becoming president after its incorporation. My story would not be complete without commenting on his exceptional qualities. Aside from his engineering ability, he was the fairest, most decent, and most compassionate executive I encountered, a true gentleman in word and deed. He set the tone for his organization and its leaders who followed him. I was a Jew and an English-speaking architect working for a Québécois company in an increasingly nationalist environment that encouraged separation from Canada. Other architects of impeccable pedigree coveted projects I designed for SNC and made it known. Camille Dagenais was loyal to me. He recognized no discrimination, whether based on colour, gender, religion, political orientation, or ethnic origin. He judged on merit. His staff, including senior executives, was multiracial and multilingual. I knew employees who had become incapacitated but were never cast out; there was always something found for them to do. I had many clients during fifty years in the maelstrom of a practice, but no one I admired more. He was a *mensch*.

★ ★ ★

My creations had to respect different cultures, lifestyles, traditions, and aesthetic preferences and be compatible with available materials, construction equipment, and levels of competence Remote sites necessitated their own construction materials, and techniques.

Challenges were not lacking. During my career, my English-speaking office slowly, but inexorably, adopted French, calculators replaced slide rules, computer-assisted design did away with pencils, metric measure superseded Imperial units, building codes proliferated and mutated out of recognition, the sixteen-volume Sweet's Catalogue of building materials that occupied an entire bookshelf shrank to a few diskettes, the Quebec Civil Code was re-written. And, along with other Québécois, we survived a few political crises. The ground shifted constantly under our feet.

Buildings were increasingly dictated by environmental and safety issues; some construction materials and systems proved faulty, thereby gratifying an army of lawyers; litigation proliferated. Insurance was invoked against every conceivable risk to ourselves, our clients and to the public, and few architects or engineers could read, much less understand the convoluted conditions composed in the microscopic type favoured by the legal community. As my experience grew, I was retained to resolve some of the resulting problems for others and acquired a modest following in forensic circles.

I knew a project was successful when a client boasted: "Look at what I designed." And I knew it was a failure—and there were some—when the client said: "Look what my architect made for me."

Every job was a story in itself, an amalgam of pride, frustration, joy, and despair when achieved, or of dark disappointment when canceled. I never, ever, regretted my choice. Perhaps some of my clients did.

I foresaw none of this when I launched my career. Life was a university that never closed its doors.

Growing Wings

My six years of university had been interspersed with summers and holidays of work in offices and on construction sites. I had experience, health, ambition, and a knack for learning quickly; first, though, I wanted to see the world that had been closed to me by the war that had just ended.

Travel abroad was now possible and I booked myself on a tour to Israel, then newly founded and victorious in a struggle for survival. I was to travel with a group that would spend one month on a kibbutz and another touring the minuscule country. But tragedy struck. Marcus, my father's brother, the husband of my mother's sister, and co-founder of the family business, died. He was fifty-three when he was taken by one of the cancers that plagued both sides of our family. We were shaken. Ma thought it inappropriate for me to leave home, even for a short time; we had to circle the wagons, to share the grief. It was one of the few times I defied her. But I couldn't abandon the adventure.

The day after graduation, I met our group at the ship. They were all young women from Toronto, university students, and far, far more sophisticated than my inexperienced self. We were bound for Cherbourg, thence by rail to Paris and Marseilles, our port of embarkation for Haifa. Along the way, our ship would take on immigrants making their way to the newly liberated Holy Land.

In Paris, our tour leader fell ill and I was delegated to shepherd the group to the kibbutz. Leading a dozen recalcitrant, spoiled young ladies with more than an eye for the lads was a saga in itself. They accurately sized me up for what I was: a socially backward Montreal bumpkin with an untried, barely dry architectural diploma. I didn't exist. They had better pickings among the virile ship's crew and the more attractive of the immigrants aboard our vessel.

We settled in at Kfar Blum, a kibbutz on the banks of the biblical River of Jordan, north of the Galilee, not far from Lebanon. In Israel, nothing was distant, large, or wide. If the roads hadn't been so narrow, winding, and choked with traffic, towns and cities would have been minutes from each other. So-called mountains, except for Mount Harmon, were modest hillocks. The fabled Jordan was a few yards wide and could readily be waded.

We rose from our tents at dawn and picked crops as they ripened. Cucumbers were in season; they grew on the ground. We walked bent double until tomatoes matured. Tomatoes grew on vines and we walked erect again. Then sunflowers: they towered over us and we bent their stalks to harvest their flowers. We learned that bees had a taste for their nectar and were enraged when disturbed; our work was never dull.

Fish were raised in artificial lagoons. We shovelled feed over the water from rowboats, scooped up our writhing piscatorial crop, and iced them for sale. When grain ripened, we stood in blinding dust as the harvester cut the stalks that we baled. It was hot, dirty labour. Weeks passed uneventfully; our group coalesced, became friends, sweated and bathed together in the muddy Jordan, and subsisted on vegetables considered unfit for sale. All went well—almost.

Awakening one morning, I knew that I was deathly ill. I could only stagger; my head burned and spun. I was delirious. An ambulance took me to a hospital in Tiberius, facing the Sea of Galilee. Doctors fluttered around me. My world disintegrated into blurred hallucinations. After a week my fever subsided, leaving me enervated, with double vision, able only to creep along walls. Doctors conducted groups of interns to my bedside, gesticulating, babbling in German, describing my mysterious symptoms: "Ja, er zet dupple—ja, dupple" (He sees double—yes, double). The consensus: polio or encephalitis; it made no difference. There was no treatment for either. That was my punishment for leaving the family at a time of crisis. I don't know how Ma did it, but it increased her reputation for omnipotence.

My tour companions visited me at my sickbed; from their awed expressions it could have been my deathbed. They pronounced messages of good cheer, but shook their heads hopelessly, brimming with sympathy, and departed. I never heard from any of them again.

My head cleared, my vision slowly corrected itself, and I lurched about, clinging to walls until my strength gradually returned.

In front of my tent in Kfar
Blum, just a week before
my bout of polio.

Meanwhile, I busily wrote letters home to cover the period of my illness. I told my parents nothing, not a word. I was consistently cheerful, full of news; I swore visitors and staff to secrecy.

And I resolved to learn Hebrew. My *Pesach* seders and bar-mitzvah studies had provided me with some low-level reading capability; understanding was another matter. Taking a Hebrew dictionary, I selected about fifty commonly used nouns starting with each letter, and set about memorizing them, beginning with the first letter, *aleph*. After two weeks I was released from the hospital, feeble, but with an excellent command of words up to *mem*, halfway along the alphabet. I could carry on a truncated noun-based conversation; verbs were conveyed by body language, facial expressions, and hands.

My next stop was a recovery home, where I completed the alphabet. I could limp around comfortably and decided to stay on. My letters home related, truthfully this time, that I had relocated to Jerusalem, found employment as a draftsman in a small architectural office, was rooming comfortably with an Israeli family, and was seriously considering taking up residence. My modest salary was enough for a young bachelor with inexpensive tastes. Without Ma to safeguard me, I could feast every night on sausages, sauerkraut, and beer.

My Hebrew vocabulary grew to include architectural terms and I became proficient in my work. Construction materials were scarce and designs could include only what was available. It was challenging, stimulating, and exciting.

Pressure from home to return mounted. My stay had stretched from two months to seven and the family feared that I was becoming too comfortable in the Promised Land. Ma was increasingly disabled by that relentless tumour in her spine. I had left home against her wishes and I couldn't defy her again; I still limped with the consequences of my last betrayal. It was time to go.

At the end of the year, I regretfully bade farewell to Israel.

In and Out of Practice

Now that I was home, decisions had to be made about my career. I returned to the architect who had employed me during summers and holiday breaks in my university years. He was pleased to have me, and I was happy to gain experience and earn sixty-five dollars each and every week. I had grander ideas in mind and, after some months, I asked about my future. Recognizing in me a willing and fastidious worker but a timid and naive businessman, he promised a partnership—sometime, somehow.

His practice, carried on the wave of post-war construction, was busy, and I soon directed a small staff. It didn't escape me that many of his projects ended in recrimination, even lawsuits. Also, he devoted most of his time entertaining potential clients at watering holes that served no water. But my vision was impaired because my nose was close to the grindstone. I wanted that partnership and applied myself unsparingly to learning the business.

I vividly remember the first time my boss sent me to inspect work in progress: it was a restaurant. The workers were grizzled Italians who were highly skilled but poorly paid contractors, spending their lives balanced on scaffolds laying bricks, or perched on ladders plastering walls, or on their knees finishing concrete floors. They saw a fresh-faced boy of an architect arriving to supervise their work; it was obvious that I had clean fingernails and had never worn overalls. I strolled onto the job with my roll of blueprints and promptly stepped onto a floor of wet terrazzo, an amalgam of marble chips in a cement bed; I had ruined a day's work. The workers were armed with trowels; I left quickly.

I had much to learn, and my employer's practice, if not profitable, was entertaining. He promoted his practice at expensive bars, bringing him into contact with their owners—fine fellows, jovial, witty, and shrewd, who had other, less reputable, sources of income: illegal gambling houses known as bookmakers. One such bookie joint was directly across the hall from our office. I designed it according to their specifications; no handbooks carried information on this building type. The premises consisted of a reception area administered by a decorative, alert young lady who admitted customers by pressing an under-carpet button. A door, cunningly hidden by mouldings, opened into a large room lined with counters that supported a collection of Damon Runyonesque characters nibbling smoked meat sandwiches and taking bets over any one of thirty phones. The action was continuous around the clock.

Our drafting room had six workstations and usually one to three employees. To impress a client, I would step across the hall, invite several habitués into our drafting room, and prop one against each of our tables, pencil in hand. At the critical moment, my employer would fling open his door, exposing the client to a full team ostensibly producing drawings. It was impressive. Once the door closed again, our "architects" returned to their bets and smoked meat.

I pressed for the promised partnership. It was finally arranged that I would have a one-third interest in the architectural practice only, but my partner would devote his time to housing development, a highly profitable business for shrewd operators. It happened that the practice earned little, and the construction scheme, requiring more than attendance at restaurants and bars, went nowhere. After a year, it occurred to even a financial dunce like myself that I didn't need a partner. I could starve independently.

I told him. "I want to leave, but I'll stay as long as you need me to complete any work, to train a successor, and to make the transition as painless as possible, all in accordance with any schedule that would suit you."

He explained his position. "Give me the keys. Get out." I left.

He owed me more than two thousand dollars, a princely sum in those days. Repayment was not his priority. With little faith in legal recourse, I went to C. Davis Goodman, Montreal's pre-eminent Jewish architect with considerable influence in the association to which all architects belonged. He was in his seventies, ruthlessly ethical, and very impressive. Through his mediation, I obtained much of what was due.

C.D., as he was known, asked me what was next for me.

"Well, my family has a home," I told him. "I'll open an office in their basement."

"Listen, my boy," he said (I was all of twenty-five), "I have spare space in my office. Use the premises, the telephone, chat with the secretary, ask questions. No charge."

It was a generous invitation, especially welcome as I had almost no income. I moved in. Slowly, clients came. I renovated kitchens, finished basements—nothing was too small. I'd designed many low-cost houses with my previous partner and began to acquire a reputation among developers for knowing how to build economically. As my cash flow improved, I insisted that C.D. accept rent. He reluctantly agreed to a modest sum.

Time passed. I was earning something that didn't excite laughter when I made a bank deposit. I again turned to C.D. "I appreciate what you have done for me. However, I have reached the point where I need an employee of my own and, as Ma used to say, 'One guest doesn't bring another.' I appreciate your generosity and consideration, but it's time for me to leave."

C.D. reflected a moment. "How would you like to be my partner?"

The sky fell on me. I knew that C.D.'s practice had passed its glory days. He had never had a partner and had reached the stage when clients of his generation were retiring, dying, or forgetting his name, along with their own. He had no successor and could use my energy and ambition. I could only profit from his experience and connections. I faced a dilemma.

Since I graduated, I had been regarded with more respect by Pa. I knew how to build. Pa had never lifted a hammer and a screwdriver was beyond him, even with an instruction manual, but he had business acumen and foresight. I was enraptured by design and couldn't see beyond the point of my pencil.

Pa had a plan. "The city needs housing. Apartments haven't been upgraded, or even maintained, since the war began. I have money to invest. I'll buy older buildings; you renovate, rent, and manage them. There's a market."

Of course, he was right. But, for reasons clear to any psychiatrist, I was very reluctant. I didn't want to work for Pa. I never had. He was a good man, fair, quiet spoken, prudent. Perhaps I harboured resentment at being controlled by anyone, maybe I dreaded risking his money, or his approval. But he persevered. He bought thirteen "doors," as apartments in multi-family buildings were described in those days. I negotiated and collected the rent, directed repairs, kept records, paid bills—and my stomach was in knots. If the furnace broke down, I froze with my tenants; if the garage door jammed, so did my intestines. After a couple of years I prevailed on him to sell the property. He regretfully parted with it; I left it with intense relief. It was irrational on my part—inexcusable. Pa had been right. At my insistence opportunities had been neglected.

A partnership with C.D. would, I feared, arouse the same feelings. I would be junior partner for a long time, taking direction from a quasi-father; I would never be free. I had already suffered through a failed junior partnership. I desperately needed independence, but the temptation was powerful. With a full heart, I thanked C.D. but refused. With real regret, I left. It was the right choice for me, and we remained friends.

One, Two, Three—Lift-off!

I launched myself into practice. I had to see what I was made of. Along with Hy Tolchinsky, another neophyte architect, and my cousin, David Rabin, a newly licenced land surveyor, I rented an office; we shared all expenses. The building was new, the rent affordable: seventy-five dollars a month, including electricity. All the other tenants wore white: several were doctors, two were pharmacists, one a dentist, and others operated a beauty parlour. The walls were thin, and I could hear the obstetrician in the adjoining office examining expectant mothers.

We hired a receptionist-secretary; she was attractive, ensuring that clients arrived well before their appointments—but inept. She filed accounts receivable, accounts payable, taxes, and petty cash under M. "M is for money," she explained.

The post-war construction boom was underway. There were plenty of clients, but also plenty of architects. Battling stiff competition, I had established a clientele among entrepreneurs who styled themselves as builders. Of course, they knew nothing about building. But they knew to buy land with nothing down. They knew how to obtain architectural drawings on credit, to pre-sell or pre-rent space based on these drawings, to obtain temporary financing based on these commitments, and to launch a project, mortgaged comfortably above the construction cost, all without investing a red cent.

They were familiar with risks. Many had survived the war using only their wits, when loss of nerve could mean death. In Canada, the penalty for launching an unsuccessful project without money was trivial; one could only go bankrupt—that is, lose money that one never had anyway. And the rewards were great. Many became very wealthy. That they couldn't differentiate between a brick and shingle was immaterial—that's what they paid architects for. But they didn't pay very much: ten dollars was top price for each house built. They sprawled in tracts across farmland that was paved into suburbs with unmapped, unnamed streets; I had no idea where, and had to find them to count them.

Similar creative thinking was applied to apartments, shopping malls, office buildings—anything buildable with borrowed funds. Although I was busy, I could see that, as far as architectural services were involved, this road was not paved with gold. It was hardly paved at all.

My previous partner had a client who moved in government circles. He liked my work. When I opened my office, he became one of my earliest patrons. That was my introduction to the netherworld of patronage and politics.

In those halcyon days Quebec was autocratically governed by a party called the Union Nationale. Under its rule, the provincial government never troubled itself with competitive bids for public works. Contracts were divided among a coterie of supporters who returned these favours in ways no longer conducted openly. My client, nameless for obvious reasons, had been a humble supplier of gravel that he delivered in his one-truck fleet. He had the foresight to make a modest but timely political contribution to Maurice Duplessis, the then-to-be premier. When his candidate came to power, my client was favoured each year with several major construction projects: a bridge, a government office building, or a satisfying equivalent. Cost and technical capability were not factors, but the project had to be delivered on time, as promised to the electorate. Ridings that did not elect a member of the party in power found their rivers uncrossed by bridges and highways unpaved within their boundaries. Those who opposed Duplessis' policies too vigorously, or who had "subversive" political or religious affiliations, had their premises padlocked.

I designed buildings that my patron erected for several important ministries. The Korean War was in progress and steel construction materials were embargoed. Such was my client's influence that beams, columns, and rebar for his buildings were never a day late. Although such practices are no longer as flagrant, these and other manipulations that I witnessed in later years provided interesting lessons in the uses of power and the transparency of governments.

I Become Industry-ous

Then, my fortunes turned. A friend, Dan Hadekel, an engineer by profession, was made vice-president of Henry J. Kaiser, an immense American conglomerate that built ships, smelted metals, concentrated ores, refined whatever was unrefined, and pulled industrial levers that spun the planet. Dan was to be stationed in Montreal to manage construction of an iron-ore concentrator deep in the wilderness several hundred miles north of Sept-Îles. Kaiser needed an architect. Was I interested? Certainly. I knew what iron was and I could concentrate. An architect arrived from California to interview me.

"What's your experience with sub-arctic design and construction?" he asked.

I fleetingly considered mentioning a winter cottage that I had designed in the Laurentians, but discarded the notion.

"None," I admitted.

"How about roofing systems under extreme conditions?"

"None."

"And your knowledge of ore extraction, crushing, and treatment?"

"None."

"You're hired. Everyone else thinks they know. They don't. We'll train you."

Built in the mid-1950s, the concentrator cost sixty million. It was a vast step up from the small warehouses and minor shopping centres that I had heretofore designed. I had much to learn, in a hurry, and I did. Before long, I knew how to concentrate iron ore and design appropriate buildings for the process and its workers. In a spirit of true cooperation I agreed to not compete with them in concentrating iron. By the time I retired, I had forsworn smelting aluminum, rolling stainless steel, refining zinc, gold, and oil, and producing magnesium, cement, glass fibre, paper, pharmaceuticals, plastics, concrete masonry, and almost all building materials, as well as many chemicals that I couldn't spell. Many careers were closed to me.

I undertook Kaiser's project with great enthusiasm. At the end of the first month, I submitted my bill. It was promptly paid, and in full. No haggling. It was a revelation. I hadn't known that clients like that existed. My world opened up.

Kaiser was an American company. I had my first taste of the tendency of foreign investors to disregard advice of local architects and engineers to respect Canadian conditions when designing their industrial projects. It was commonly understood among designers: "You can always tell an American—but you can't tell him much." The deadly combination of cold and moisture could deteriorate walls and roofs, create impossible working conditions, and heave unprotected structures resting on frozen soil. The National Research Council was always available for consultation, and I learned rapidly; penalties for ignorance or carelessness were high.

My iron ore concentrator would use sixty thousand gallons of water per minute. An above-grade, uninsulated pipeline was to be built to a large lake nine miles distant. In vain we warned of sub-zero temperatures. The first winter produced a nine-mile icicle; iron ore stored in silos froze solid and had to be loosened by explosives; walls and roofs of structures housing high-humidity processes were lined with ice. Similar blunders were made by other foreign companies despite our emphatic advice.

I made no grievous errors, and one concentrator led to another. I was emboldened to approach a growing engineering company with the cumbersome name of Surveyer, Nenniger & Chenevert, later shortened to SNC. They were cool to architects. Their fleeting experiences with our profession had been unhappy: architects were arrogant, built monuments to themselves, argued incessantly, spent money on non-essentials, and knew little and cared less about mundane matters such as structure, heating, electricity, and production processes. Engineers preferred to prepare the plans and pay an architect to validate them. Our architectural association frowned on its members collaborating with non-architects; it debased both professions.

Recognizing some truth in these mutual recriminations, I made a proposal to SNC: "Give me your dirtiest project to design. Pay me by the hour. I will design all the buildings to accommodate your process requirements, and stamp and seal my drawings. If, at any time, for any reason, you are dissatisfied—fire me. That's our contract." It was less than a page.

The project was successful, and was the forerunner of a collaboration that continues until today. Our joint ventures run into billions of dollars, and our recognition with other industries grew accordingly. We promised and we delivered.

SNC selected their "dirtiest project": a zinc refinery near Montreal for an American company; it was not to be heated. Again I was confronted with a client who wanted to save money in the wrong places. I pleaded with the project manager. He compromised, agreeing to insulate and heat only the employee facilities.

I visited the refinery in February. The plant was filled with large open tanks side by side, separated by narrow walkways. Dense fumes rising from the witch's brew bubbling in those tanks into the frigid air reduced visibility to zero; employees circulating on walkways blew whistles to advertise their presence or risk being hit by approaching workers carrying pipes. But few employees were walking anywhere. They were huddled in their heated washrooms. By the following winter an adequate heating system was in place.

Every industry was fair game for our firm's growing expertise. Shell Canada, whose emissions perfumed the city from east to west, favoured me with a commission for a small loading dock. For this I travelled the length of the island of Montreal daily. Across the road from Shell's facility was one belonging to Texaco, another oil giant. I told the manager that since I was already working in the district, I could service his company. Texaco needed a small office building. Texaco led to Gulf Oil, then to Imperial Oil. Soon I had cornered the refinery market. Eventually I graduated to Sarnia, with major work for Sunoco. The air smelled sweeter with each contract.

As Pa had said, "Don't wait for clients to come to you; go to them and design what they need." I knocked on many doors and more than a few opened. That was how I built my business, one industry at a time—the dirtier the better. There was less competition. Soon, thanks to Pa's philosophy, I was designing everything that started with an A: A smelter, A refinery, A rolling mill, A concentrator . . .

The Partnership Ball: My First Dance

The early years of my practice were filled with modest projects, but the acquisition of major industrial clients required my full attention. In 1955, my third year of practice, I had taken my chief and only draftsman, Nathan Schertzer, as a partner, the first of several who came and went over the next fifty years. Nat was quiet, industrious, and, above all, without temperament. He agreed with everybody. Mostly he busied himself with our crowd of capricious and greedy builders. He was eminently accommodating, accepting any excuse for late, partial, or even non-payment of our hard-earned fees, paltry as they were. When I remonstrated with Nat, he agreed with me too. When his builders demanded changes to completed and accepted plans, he smiled and served. But he was so pleasant that it was impossible to be angry with him.

He had only one discordant trait: he jogged. Those were the days of fitness worship and he seduced me into going daily to the neighbourhood YMHA. At lunch, we cheerfully exchanged problems, disappointments, and frustrations with a pack of health-crazed enthusiasts. The whole outing was spoiled by the need to lurch—sweating, aching, breathless—around the gym in winter and the park in summer. It reminded me of my school days.

Nat was at my side, constantly encouraging me: "Keep it up. You'll get your second wind."

"I haven't gotten my first," I would gasp.

"Your endorphins will kick in," he assured me. I had no breath to inform him that no one in our family had ever produced a single endorphin.

But Nat gloried in it. He bounded along, fresher at the finish than I was at the start. Almost a half-century later, but no longer a partner, he still bounds along, looking twenty years younger than his age, a jogger with a contented smile. How I don't envy him!

While I went about soliciting and producing industrial projects, Nat remained loyal to his builders and they to him. And no wonder: we lost money on every one of them. Our industrial practice flourished.

I added a third partner. Marcus Scoler was young, ambitious, a hard worker, and a tireless business promoter, attracting commercial and smaller industrial clients. He longed to expand our horizons and introduced another partner, Tom Gluck, an "inside" man, to manage production.

Our business grew. We were well established with engineering consultants and with major national and international companies investing and building plants in Canada.

"We're smarter than our clients," Marcus argued. "Why aren't we as rich? Why not develop projects ourselves? Build, rent, sell. In no time you'll be able to relax at home and write your memoirs."

He didn't reckon with my visceral fear of putting my signature to astronomical bank loans and mortgages, wooing tenants, and chasing late rental payments. Risk aversion was my hobby, my vocation, my obsession. I couldn't bear haggling with contractors and suppliers. I would have none of it. He dreamed of successful speculations; I had nightmares of bankruptcy. Reich, Schertzer, Scoler & Gluck, Architects were a winning team—for the time being. But clouds were gathering.

In 1976, the Parti Québécois, a political entity devoted to separation of Quebec from Canada, came to power. There would be a referendum, perhaps another: as many as would be required for Quebec to vote itself out of Canada.

We were nervous. Jewish history was replete with horrendous consequences of nationalism. Although our fears may have been exaggerated, the Holocaust was a living memory. Many Jews left and many of our children sought careers elsewhere, taking their financial acumen and talents to western Canada or the United States.

Locally, construction projects were cancelled in mid-hammer stroke, excavations were abandoned. Investment dried. Money flowed out of the province in armoured trucks. Everything was frozen. We sat around our suddenly silent office and plotted.

Marcus, the energizer, put it to us: "Quebec is dead. Ontario is alive and kicking and will profit from investment lost from here. I'll travel to Toronto every Monday morning, promote projects, return on Friday; you'll produce the work in Montreal."

And so it was. After a year of frenetic travel and promotion, Marcus demonstrated that it was now feasible, indeed, necessary, to open a Toronto branch. He would sell his recently completed Montreal home and relocate. Tom would accompany him to operate the office while he drummed up even more business. We agreed. I was left with Nat; he jogged and the office limped. His builders had fled.

Before long Marcus advanced another step. "We're profitable in Toronto and will be even more so. Montreal will die. Join us in Toronto. If not, we'll keep our profits; you retain yours."

I had no interest in leaving Montreal. It held all my family, friends, business connections, and my academic milieu. My home was here, life was pleasant and working in French was not daunting—in fact, it opened opportunities for us. Toronto had no bagels worthy of the name and smoked meat was unknown. I would stay; the profits would accrue to our respective offices. And so it was.

The situation between our two branches became complicated. Calculation of costs and division of profits were not simple. The respective provincial architectural associations wanted to know who and what we were and our insurer asked questions. Finally it became clear that it was easier, cleaner, and less distracting to separate completely. We did, without rancour, and remain friendly to this day.

Now I was back with only Nat. The business climate had chilled, if not frozen; our world had changed. We needed a French face.

Of course, we could not ignore the growing francization in Quebec. When I had started my practice, site meetings were invariably conducted in English, even if most of the participants were French-speaking. The reverse was now true. Technical literature was increasingly published in French. The bulletin of our provincial association gradually eliminated English. In public, English was degraded in size and visibility, and it eventually disappeared from commercial signs.

Back to School, Teaching

By the mid-1960s, it was clear that I needed to work in French. Teaching in that language seemed the shortest way to learn it without interrupting my architectural practice. Respecting a family tradition of profiting from adverse situations, I sought a job in a French college. I found a position at the Institut de technologie de Montréal, where students graduated as technicians trained to assist architects and building contractors in their duties. Recalling remnants of French grammar acquired in high school and memorizing key words in advance of each lecture, I crept through the curriculum, gathering fluency as I went.

Soon I was comfortable in my new environment. It opened a whole new world for me. Heretofore, I had dwelled in a city populated by citizens who, if they spoke English at all, had foreign accents; they were strangers to me. In a surprisingly short time they became real people, with all shades of emotion, ambitions, and capabilities, fun-loving, romantic, artistic—all had been hidden from me, as I had been hidden from them.

In the late 1960s, a provincial college system with two streams, general and vocational, was established and the Institut was folded into the new CEGEP du Vieux Montréal. Armed with a licence to teach in French, I was asked to write the architectural curriculum and to direct the Technologie d'architecture program. But I knew that the duties of a director included attending interminable meetings, administering budgets that were insufficient, fending off unions, mediating the petty jealousies of quarrelsome teachers, and becoming involved in college politics. In short, he did nothing. I would become a bureaucrat, await my retirement, and collect my pension. Death was preferable.

I graciously declined and was transferred to Dawson College, the first English CEGEP, where I taught Civil Technology, a program that trained technicians to assist building engineers. When I was not familiar with certain building techniques, I found guest lecturers to instruct my students on their specialties. CIL, producer of explosives for construction, assembled, in our classroom, a complete display of its blasting agents, wired together, fitted with detonators, fuses, and timers—of course, all dummies. In the midst of the presentation, the fire alarm sounded. We dutifully vacated the building and waited outside for the signal to return—and waited. Police swarmed about. There had been a bomb warning and the building was about to be searched. I made the necessary explanations. They understood, but insisted that I be the first to enter the classroom.

Dawson College did not offer an architectural technology program, because, it was explained, no students had applied; no students had applied because the program was not advertised, and it was not advertised because it didn't exist due to lack of students. Eventually enough rejects were recruited from other programs and I was mandated to establish an Architectural Technology department at a building newly constructed to house Vanier College.

I was notified at the end of July that the program would open the first week in September; it lacked only equipment, teachers, and curriculum. The Vanier Board asked, "You have four weeks before the first lecture. Is it enough time?" I had had experience with boards; I replied: "Yes, but only if the administration promises not to advise and assist." They agreed—hands off!

The next day I ordered drawing boards, drafting instruments, and teaching supplies. Then I recruited faculty. I had obtained approval to hire part-time lecturers for each specialty. By that time I had been an architect for twenty years and was well acquainted with local professionals in different disciplines. I selected those best qualified to teach structures, heating, ventilating, air conditioning, electrical services, estimating, and surveying. I reserved drafting and building construction for myself, allowing me classroom time with each student for each semester of the three-year program. I directed my new instructors to teach what they practiced every day and be prepared to work without meetings, memos, or other formalities essential for education. They only had to produce students ready to take their place in the construction industry. By the end of the month I had, with the enthusiastic co-operation of my staff, completed the curricula for all the courses.

We were ready on September 1. The eight-storey building was new and elevators had not yet been installed; we were on the top floor. Students were treated to a fitness program in addition to architectural technology.

I loved teaching. It forced me to learn details of materials and construction processes beyond what architects normally learned. Furthermore, in my industrial practice I had designed buildings used to manufacture many building materials, including polystyrene, glass fibre, aluminum, steel, zinc, cement, and pre-fabricated concrete products. With my students, I brought my students to building sites and to factories producing construction materials and laboratories that tested them.

My program had four applicants for each available space and I interviewed every candidate, selecting the best and most motivated. No doubt I misjudged some, but the quality of my graduates speaks for itself. They were eagerly recruited by the design and construction industry; several spent their entire working lives in my office. Others became professionals themselves and merited their successful careers. I treasure those days; I learned more than the students. And had more fun.

Back to School, Learning

By now, most of my work was with engineers. As an architect, I wasn't a member of that sacred calling. I had designed many major projects but my engineering skills had become outdated; my courses had been taken twenty-five years earlier. The intervening years had witnessed the advent of computers, advanced methods of management, scheduling, testing, adoption of metric units—a whole new world. When I was fifty, I enrolled at Concordia University for a master's degree in engineering—at night. My days were filled. Back in the classroom I was among a younger generation, schooled in computers and advanced mathematics. In some courses, my practical experience put me ahead of my instructors. In others, I was a neophyte.

I looked over my classmates. One in particular was very industrious. He took notes on everything: the professor talked, he wrote. I sat myself next to him and looked over his shoulder; his extensive notes were in Hebrew. He was an Israeli. He was bright, knowledgeable and, above all, amenable. We agreed to meet weekends; he tutored me in my weak subjects and I helped him in work I knew well. We partnered in our assignments. After eight years, I was a Master of Engineering. In 1985 I received my diploma amidst cheers. Why not? I was the oldest person on that stage. I was even older than the stage.

Adrift on a Computer

In the early 1980s, computer-assisted drawing (CAD) showed great promise and was on the threshold of universal acceptance within the hallowed offices of architects. Clearly, this technique would soon replace conventional drawing boards, parallel rules, set squares, and other manual drawing tools that were used to train architects and technologists in every school, including, of course, the CEGEPs. This was apparent to everyone—except educators comfortably mired in tradition and content to squabble over what not to do next.

At that point, the federal government announced that funds were to be made available to schools for computers. I immediately recruited Joe Rabinovitch, Vanier's open-minded and perceptive principal, and within days we had prepared a proposal, the first to be submitted to Ottawa. We budgeted for personal desktop computers fitted with CAD software. Our students would be given these tools and trained to use them, and with these skills they would be virtually guaranteed employment on graduation.

The government approved two million dollars. The college director, a former car salesman with an intimate lack of knowledge of education in general and architecture in particular, immediately stepped in. He allocated about half the budget to buy downtown office space for an independent training operation and spent the other half on an enormously expensive mainframe computer connected to workstations, a system that had never been installed in any architect's office in Quebec, and never would be. It was useless. Instead of having ready access to small, relatively inexpensive, flexible desktop computers, our students would travel downtown once a week to learn software that they would never see agaiI protested to no avail. I visited the Chair of the Vanier Board . As expected, she responded, "Well, you know, we have a director, and we cannot redirect directors." Clearly the grant had been wasted and the students' chances for state-of-the-art training had disappeared, I resigned. Subsequently, when the obsolescence of the system became apparent even to the director, the school reverted to appropriate equipment that I had recommended, with suitable software. By that time, I was gone, another victim of bureaucracy.

Exposure to computers opened my eyes to their enormous potential. CAD-generated architectural and engineering drawings were exploding in popularity. Drawings produced by these disciplines were linked, and ultimately information between design offices was transmitted by cable. Pencils disappeared from offices; it was simpler and faster to create, manipulate, and transmit digitized information.

Plans, heretofore laid out on paper in two dimensions, could be transformed into three-dimensional renderings. Viewers of the computer screen could virtually tour a building room by room, see it from any vantage point, walk around its walls, and see surfaces in any colour they chose. Drawings of building systems could be combined to display any conflicts or anomalies before they reached the construction phase. Drawings were transmitted to our printers by wire. It was all revolutionary. Latecomers to the digital age, like myself, seldom achieved full familiarity with this technology. In my younger days I had been an excellent draftsman with pen and pencil; now, I would be unemployable. Fortunately, I had reached a stage where my value lay in soliciting work, preparing design sketches, and supervising production. I happily left the new digital world to the competent fingers of fresh, eager, talented youngsters.

However, I knew what computers could produce in the hands of these baby-faced geniuses and looked for ways to profit from this marvellous technology. I found several.

Manufacturers of construction materials publicized their products in bulky and expensive printed catalogues distributed free to designers. I visualized making the same information available on diskettes, with each product incorporated into the appropriate building system: for example, different forms of insulation could be installed in many different types of walls and roofs. All variations and their combinations could be recorded on a diskette and distributed at a fraction of the printed cost. Relevant details would be retrieved by designers from the diskette and added to computerized drawings with a single keystroke and an enormous saving in time. We prepared such diskettes and demonstrated them to manufacturers. They were enthralled, and contracts followed. After a couple of years, they realized how easy it was to prepare these diskettes themselves and our business disappeared. But it was successful while it lasted.

The Sweets Catalogue of construction materials consisted of at least sixteen massive volumes; every architect's office had a set. I proposed to digitize the information onto diskettes. The Sweets people refused, politely hiding their smiles. Inevitably they joined the digital world; they had to, or disappear like the dinosaurs.

I had another inspiration: several fire fighters had been killed when a burning roof collapsed beneath them. Had they had known the construction of the roof, they would not have died. It leaped to mind that technology permitted drawings of existing buildings to be scanned, modified with additional information, and recorded. A municipality could readily digitize drawings of buildings in its permit files, and add or modify data relevant to fire fighters, such as type and location of their fire protection systems, electric panels, stairways, building structure, and dedicated elevators. These data could be readily available to fire fighters from computers mounted in their vehicles. This idea was deemed too expensive.

Teaching and developing the architectural curriculum for all CEGEPs allowed me to accumulate a comprehensive reference library. I attended legal seminars to acquire a background in construction law. My lectures, some of them four hours long, left students exhausted, but allowed me to prepare useful resource material. Putting all this together and recognizing that the financial acumen of developers and builders often exceeded their technical capability, I customized seminars for them. At last, even they could understand the causes and prevention of problems afflicting building envelopes, failures of building materials and assemblies, and much more.

These ventures aside, I was teaching full time and practicing full time. The latter required attention. Our world had shifted. Marcus and Tom were gone. I had Nat, who, in the absence of his builder clientele, jogged. Finally he had to choose between his running shoes and full-time attention to the practice—in French. He chose the shoes.

I turned my attention to solidifying my practice to better meet my market. This would involve transforming the office into a fully French-speaking entity while serving our American clients in English. Another task would be to employ my experience and training to advise on quality control of design and settlement of construction-related disputes.

Tiptoeing Through Building Codes

Design of large, complex industrial projects had become my specialty. Every process and occupancy presented unique risks to the safety of its occupants. Permits, based on construction drawings, were issued by different government offices to confirm conformity with codes. These included, but were not limited to zoning, fire protection, structure, mechanical and electrical services, energy conservation, barrier-free access for the disabled, noise and vibration control, and much more. However, it was impossible to draft laws to cover every aspect of every industry: metals, chemicals, paper, cement, explosives, pharmaceuticals—the list is endless. All involved risks of different types and magnitude.

Obtaining a building permit was, and remains, a greater challenge to the architect than designing the building, or supervising its construction, or even collecting the fee. To negotiate a permit for a building of unusual size, configuration or occupancy was especially onerous; it required long, tedious, and frustrating negotiations with bureaucrats, representatives of cities or provinces, or federal departments, or combinations thereof.

Bureaucrats are a special breed: they infest every government department at every level. They are paid for their ability to say "no." What's the use of a bureaucrat who says yes? He's redundant, not needed. Therefore, a bureaucrat must be someone who can find somewhere, somehow, an interpretation of some regulation, however obscure, to frustrate the construction of the project.

Industrial buildings are not usually subjected to aesthetic review, but the great variety of processes and equipment often create conditions not covered by building codes. An aluminum smelter more than a half-mile long and a quarter-mile wide, enclosing about five million square feet of open space without a single firewall and employing a thousand workers, presents limitless opportunities for "no." Hence, processing a permit is a long, arduous process, akin to rabbis disputing fine points of the Talmud. Eventually, though, even the bureaucrat becomes bored or sees an opportunity to frustrate a larger project and moves on.

I won only one notable victory in my many battles with the hierarchy. Energy-conservation codes required all walls to be insulated, even those enclosing occupancies virtually open to the weather. Storage buildings with large doors are an example. The lower portion of these walls was usually built of concrete to withstand vehicular impact. Insulating these sections was a needless expense that I undertook to eliminate, claiming they weren't walls at all, but windows.

The bureaucrat argued, "But sir, but what you claim are windows made of concrete."

"True," I countered. "They are made of concrete to withstand impact of trucks outside and fork lifts inside. Which article of the Code prohibits concrete windows?"

He couldn't find one; I received the permit. I used this ploy for three years until I was notified that concrete windows would no longer be accepted. I gained such notoriety for this ploy that I was invited to serve on a committee of the National Research Council responsible for creating codes.

To shorten this long and dismal tale, I was the best qualified in our firm to negotiate permits. In this capacity, I often conferred with Antoine, a senior bureaucrat of rare competence. He actually understood the intent of codes and sincerely sought solutions, equivalencies, and common-sense approaches to problems not foreseen in the regulations. I spoke to him.

"Antoine, you are unique. You seek to solve, not create, problems. But you're in the wrong place. We both know that architects are no match for permit departments; far from it. We need a code expert to review drawings before their completion and negotiate for the permit. We need someone who speaks *bureaucration*, who understands the bureaucratic mentality. You are that man. Come, leave your comfortable office. Join me. You'll sell your incomparable code expertise and I'll contribute my construction experience. The field is vast, the opportunities limitless. Codes will get thicker, denser, less comprehensible. Let's build a practice together."

In 1986 Antoine and I founded Technorm. I worked with him for twenty years. Today, his thirty-person staff serves design professionals, building owners, and municipalities. As building codes grow more complex and design professionals assume increasing responsibility for meeting them, his special expertise has grown from being useful to being essential.

I soon learned that attorneys fattened on construction-related conflicts and injuries to building users. These involved every conceivable combination of design professionals, contractors, manufacturers or suppliers of materials, and, of course, the general public. Although lawyers fixated on demands for damages, they were woefully ignorant of the technical aspects of these claims. They needed experienced, credible, and literate architects who could study each situation and prepare a report clear enough for the simplest legal mind, even a judge, to understand.

I felt that I was well qualified, and I soon had a thriving sideline dealing with claims for latent defects, delays, charges for contract changes, allegations of design or construction errors or omissions, safety of premises, and countless other real or imagined problems involving very substantial claims. It is a matter of public record that many public institutions cost several times their original estimate, and I was often retained to adjudicate additional fees demanded by their designers.

To further my competence, I completed a course in arbitration at the McGill University Law School and ultimately became a certified arbitrator. Because this procedure was quicker, simpler, and cheaper than a court trial, it was resisted by lawyers and never gained wide acceptance.

If the matter could not be mediated, I would appear before a judge, where my prematurely gray hair, qualifications, and list of completed projects lent weight to my testimony. I issued reports in over four hundred such cases and can boast that most were settled out of court, occasionally to the satisfaction of the contestants.

My education and experience gained me a modest reputation in dealing with technical matters. I was retained by the Association des finisseurs de béton du Québec (Concrete Finishers' Association of Quebec) to create standard specifications for their trade. Most design professionals, including me, were unfamiliar with the tools, equipment, and expertise required to achieve durable floors within acceptable tolerances; such a standard would ensure fair bidding practices. The trade was dominated by Italians; they had imported skills honed over the centuries dating from Roman times. They also imported their language, and we communicated in fractured English and French, using our hands when tongues failed us.

I reviewed with their workers exactly how and what they did at every stage of pouring, curing, floating, trowelling, and hardening concrete, and identified options for different building occupancies. Their explanations were as vague as my mother's descriptions of her recipes: a touch of this and a pinch of that. For example: the final operation involved trowelling floor surfaces. Too much trowelling brought water to the top, reducing resistance to abrasion; too little trowelling left the floor unpolished and more difficult to maintain. I asked a veteran worker, How does one decide? "Its'a easy," he said, with a thick Italian accent. "You take'a the trowel, you hit'a the blade on the floor and listen to the tune. That'sa how you know!" That, and thirty years on his hands and knees, wielding a trowel in his calloused fist.

I wrote the book and treasure the experience. I know how to finish a floor: hire an experienced Italian.

The Partnership Ball: My Second Dance

I was now partner in an additional business, but the architectural practice still lacked a French-speaking presence. It needed a young, energetic architect whose accent unmistakably placed his ancestors on the Plains of Abraham at the side of General Montcalm: *un vrai Québécois, pure laine, de souche.*

I had such a young man on my staff—Jean. He leaped at the chance. In 1980, we became partners.

He complemented me. He could lay the whip on the staff, fire incompetents without compunction, knock on doors hitherto closed, sling the French slang replete with humour incomprehensible to me, drink with the boys, and authoritatively discuss the merits of beers, talk of ice fishing with affection, distinguish subtleties of wines, ride snowmobiles—everything I could not do. As he frequently told me. *"Je suis Latin, vous êtes cartesien,"* by which he meant that he was a romantic, as driven by his emotions as I was governed by logic. Jean saw himself as a dashing, romantic cavalier and me as a plodding, calculating, cerebral planner.

Our practice flourished, but not quickly enough to satisfy Jean. He proposed that we expand, starting with a northern branch in Jonquière, then an eastern branch in the Gaspé—today Québec, tomorrow the world! I refused; I was not an empire builder; it was difficult enough to operate one office profitably. I preferred to produce our work in Montreal, where we were recognized, respected, and close to our major clients. Later sections describe how I diversified into related fields that benefited from my expertise: inspecting buildings, resolving construction-related disputes, applying codes, and using my engineering and pedagogical experience as a basis for seminars and courses.

One service we attempted proved less than successful. Jean and I saw a future in interior design and we recruited a decorator to operate this division. He was young, energetic, talented, aggressive—and crooked. It transpired that what he decorated best was his bank account with our fees. This ended our venture.

Jean and I made a good team—for a while.

With success, my cavalier became too dashing. He announced that he was leaving his wife and taking up with one of the secretaries. He rented an apartment, filled it with furniture, moved in, and awaited his paramour. She remained coy and at home. Jean, nonchalant on the exterior, seethed with inner Latin passion. Soon he was in the hospital with a heart attack. Further examination determined that it was stress; he had a pinched nerve. By then, my nerves were also pinched. He bought his way out of the apartment lease, sold the furniture, and returned home. The affair continued, but with new rules. He would come home in the evening and be with his wife but the days were his. And they were. He and his lady left the office together in mid-morning and returned in mid-afternoon reeking of wine. We hired an additional person to back up the wandering secretary; office morale tanked. It became intolerable.

I lunched with Jean. On the menu was a list of my demands. The affair was to stop and the secretary was to return to her keyboard. Jean acquiesced glumly. Several months later Jean notified me that I was leaving our practice and that he had concluded an arrangement with a competing architectural firm headed by two partners. He would join them, taking with him my staff and clients. It had all been arranged; he had simply neglected to inform me.

I had to decide. Jean had always taken his share of the profits from the partnership. I had left mine on deposit; this would accrue to me. Should I indeed retire? I was almost sixty and reasonably independent. I could travel, write my memoirs, teach. But it would be a defeat. No. I would fight. The mouse roared.

I called a meeting of the staff, then about twenty. Many had been my employees for years. The situation was explained, the choice was clear: remain with me, or go with Jean. Almost all were faithful to me; I was not *Latin*, not driven by emotions, and, most certainly, not romantic. My gray hair resulted from thirty-five successful years of practice, and I seemed a surer bet than Jean. My clients, too, remained loyal.

Jean left and began his attempts at empire building. Within a year, he had broken with his new partners and launched his own practice at great financial cost. A couple of years later, he came calling; he had erred, he regretted the course he had taken, and would be grateful to work with me again. I asked him when he had realized his mistake.

"On my first day," he replied. "I entered my new office, held out my hand to one of my new partners. He refused to take it. Then I knew."

By this time I had re-grouped my firm and there was no question of a partnership. However, I convinced my new associates that Jean's energy, ambition, and command of Quebec slang would facilitate penetration into the Québécois market, and that he had been cured of his romantic inclinations. For the next few years he successfully solicited clients for us in return for a share of the fees, until he left to work for an engineering company that promised more secure employment.

But Jean's departure had left me partnerless. As often happened, what appeared as a setback opened up new opportunities—but there were hurdles.

The Partnership Ball: My Third Dance

Claude was recommended to me as a potential partner. He had surmounted crippling difficulties. A teen-age alcoholic, he had barely completed high school. Alcoholics Anonymous and *chutzpah* took him into the Université de Montréal, Département d'architecture. He graduated, found employment with the Société des Alcools du Québec (SAQ, the government-run liquor board) and eventually became its chief architect. His responsibilities were not technical: he negotiated leases with building owners for locations of retail outlets.

But he longed to enter private practice and was prepared to join me. He would bring with him many important developers and building owners who had invited him to call if he ever set up his own practice. I recognized that these promises had been made when leases were being negotiated and might have little value afterward. In his important position with the Société, Claude felt indispensable and that he would be asked to continue to work for the SAQ as an independent contractor. I was not so sanguine. In my experience, when a door closes, it stays tightly shut.

Claude assured me that he was acquainted with many politically, socially, and economically well-placed Francophones through Alcoholics Anonymous. I knew many Jewophones who attended Weight Watchers. Between us, we covered a wide spectrum: the thirsty and the hungry. Plus: Claude was a card-carrying, certified *pure laine*—with roots deep in French Quebec. Minus: he spoke no English and lacked technical experience; I could readily make up for these deficiencies. I commended his courage; it was worth a try. We agreed to open a parallel practice and share the profits from any work that he developed.

Claude tried; he did his very best. He was indefatigable. But, as I feared, building owners with SAQ as tenants owed him nothing, Claude's sober friends produced no contracts, and his lack of field experience didn't improve his competitive advantage. After six months, it was clear the experiment had failed. We shook hands and parted ways. He successfully established his own practice and we remain friends.

The Partnership Ball: My Last Dance

Again, one door shut and another opened. I had made a proposal to design a project jointly with another firm of approximately the same size as mine, Stahl, Nicolaidis, Fukushima, Orton, Architects. Our offer wasn't accepted, but I was impressed with the quality and attitude of my collaborators. They, too, had considerable experience in industrial work, specializing in pharmaceutical production, research laboratories, hospitals, and food products: "clean" design. I was a "dirty" architect: ore treatment, smelters, refineries, rolling mills, paper mills, cement plants, chemical production. No one wore white in my buildings—not for long, anyway. In 1986 we merged and I had four new partners: one each from England (Nick Stahl), Greece (Costas Nicolaidis), Japan (Masa Fukushima), and Canada (Alan Orton). We named our coalition *Consultants Kenar*, that combined the name of our province (Quebec) with a Japanese word the meaning of which I have forgotten.

Our United Nations proved successful. The merger enabled us to double our production and halve our costs. Our overhead plummeted: we didn't need to duplicate accounting, specification writing, office reproduction equipment, and similar expensive necessities. Our amalgamated production capability provided further economies. Our market widened considerably. We were profitable; we had money in the bank.

In our pre-merger days, the Bank of Montreal had financed my firm. Every month it demanded to see our accounts receivable in order to decide how risk-worthy we were. Now the Bank was heavily enmeshed in loans to Third World countries whose economics and politics made repayment doubtful. I had the satisfaction of asking the bank for *its* accounts receivable. Our solvency was never again questioned.

As the firm grew, my responsibilities as senior partner became more onerous. Obtaining major projects, financing production, maintaining quality control, managing partners, associates, and staff—all essential tasks—consumed me. I no longer had the thrill of designing, of watching my buildings grow. We were successful, but life had lost its flavour. This wasn't why I'd become an architect.

★ ★ ★

In 1990 I stood on the Great Wall of China. The setting was incomparable: the sinuous rampart wound, seemingly without end, over bleak hills. It cut across a rich Far Eastern panorama. Fields were dotted with the brimmed hats of women and children bowed over rice plants, and bullocks slowly pulled wagons over muddy trails. An entire civilization so different from my own pulsed leisurely before my eyes—and I was worried about whether we would win our bid for the contract for an aluminum smelter.

I was seeing history but my mind was preoccupied with my office.

Did I really want to be harnessed to that office like a bullock, endlessly yoked with my partners to maintain what we had and acquire still more? I had a mortgage-free home and enough to live on: let another beast of burden take my place.

I made my decision.

I was sixty-three and healthy. Architecture was my life. Sadly, as senior partner I was divorced from doing what I loved: designing buildings and watching them take root and grow until they flowered into beautiful and useful structures—well, useful anyway. Instead of creating, I was soliciting work from clients, negotiating contracts, supervising design teams, and putting out the fires that always bedevil the construction process.

I was always acutely aware that I, my partners, and our heirs were personally liable for an unlimited period for errors or omissions, whether committed by us, by our staff, by contractors whose work we supervised, and by consultants we hired—the list was endless. We were at the mercy of any client with a lawyer, and no client was without one. No insurance was adequate for our exposure and no reassurance was sufficient to comfort me. I worried. Our entire family had been consistent, dedicated lifetime worriers. Could I betray family tradition?

I made mistakes along the way; there were fumbles, miscalculations, and lost opportunities, but none proved fatal. I was never sued, thereby irrefutably proving the existence of a just, Supreme Being.

I returned home and took myself off the letterhead. I would sign no more drawings and incur no further professional exposure. I'd be free to waste my time growing plants, building furniture in my workshop, and writing stories.

My partners regrouped and the firm went on. Freed from executive responsibilities, I worked another five years to direct two projects that I'd solicited and felt obligated to complete. The first involved a magnesium production facility costing almost a billion dollars and producing seventy thousand tons yearly from asbestos tailings. After completion it was found that the Chinese could process the metal much more cheaply and the plant was scrapped at considerable cost. The second project was a smelter at Lac St-Jean that turned out four hundred thousand tons of aluminum each year; it cost three billion dollars and was worth every penny; the Chinese couldn't produce it cheaper.

I couldn't design on a computer but I could sit at my desk with a squared pad and pass sketches to a dozen talented young architects whose fingers flew over their keyboards. I was an architect again. My work sputtered to an end about 1996; I said goodbye to all that.

After my departure the firm not only survived, it thrived and developed new alliances and lines of business under the direction of younger partners and associates who grew up with us. The time will come when each partner will stand on his own Great Wall of China and, if he's wise, come to the same conclusion that I did.

★ ★ ★

My career was over. I walked from the firm, sad but proud; the lights still burn at night in the offices of those who grasped the reins. But they no longer bend over drafting tables. Instead, they sit comfortably in front of glowing screens, their ink-free fingers lightly tapping keys instead of filling pens or sharpening pencils. My beautiful lettering would no longer get me a job—I would be unemployed.

My successors work hard to earn their wings. When I turned in my pencil I promised to give them all the help they needed. I'm proud to say they never needed any. I didn't die, but, like their drawings, just faded away, taking with me memories of a full life. As I said earlier: when a door closes, it remains tightly shut.

I remember summers when I sweated in a hot warehouse filling orders for schoolbooks; at the end of the five-and-a-half-day week the texts had been moved from one set of shelves to another—the work was unsatisfying. I hated every moment: I swore I'd never work again. I never did. I became an architect.

I loved designing buildings and watching their construction; I felt the thud of backhoes as they bit into the ground and dumped their loads into waiting trucks; I smelled wet concrete splashing into forms, sniffed acrid fumes of molten asphalt pouring over roofs, listened to clattering hammers and whining saws of workers framing my buildings, admired the dexterity of masons mortaring bricks into place and plasterers trowelling lime and gypsum into smooth planes. I marvelled at massive cranes swinging their loads into place to be welded together into shapes that I had conceived and I thrilled at iron workers precariously threading their way over girders no wider than their boots, and it was a long way down. I loved it all.

My Meccano and Erector sets had come to life.

As I Look Back...

Working in climates from the Arctic to the tropics, from hot deserts to dense jungles, led to many adventures. I've selected a few; they may be interesting, if not instructive.

.... almost building a Nigerian Parliament

In 1974 an international engineering firm retained me to design projects in Nigeria's Midwestern State. Its Governor, formerly an army sergeant who had been on the right side of a military coup, was warmly received by the Quebec government. Canada couldn't wait to provide foreign aid and award the resulting contracts to deserving Canadian companies. The Governor toured our province, visiting local projects that might benefit his population. A food facility that caught his attention was capable of slaughtering thousands of chickens daily, then cleaning and packaging them to emerge de-skinned, de-boned, and plastic-wrapped on sanitized cardboard trays. The Governor was interested. "Yes, Nigeria could use just such a facility."

Anyone visiting a Nigerian village would glimpse a few half-starved fowl scurrying for their lives; they'd support ten minutes of production. Similar projects were considered and discarded. Then the Governor commented favourably on the National Assembly Building in Quebec City, a fine example of nineteenth century

Second Empire French architecture clad in cut stone and topped with an ornate mansard roof; it could serve as a Parliament.

"Very impressive; we must have one." That was my mandate. I later learned that Nigeria lacked quarries and stone masons .

I inquired about the nature and functioning of the proposed Parliament. "There is no Parliament. Make one up," I was told. Hoping that appropriate materials, expertise, and equipment could be mobilized, I designed an attractive twin-towered concrete building to house an Assembly of Chiefs and a Chamber of Commoners, with plenty of committee and meeting rooms and an overpowering reception hall. I personally delivered the model and flattering photos for their consideration; they may still be moldering on some bureaucrat's shelf awaiting a free election.

Preparing for what became a couple of lengthy stays in that country, I listened to advice from several experienced travellers. I prepared a letter, conspicuously stamped, waxed and sealed with red ribbons, that ordered full cooperation with the Bearer who had important but unspecified duties to perform. I learned that I needed a *fixer* to accompany me who would clear the way with British pounds—and the way had to be cleared. All luggage would promptly declared to be overweight without benefit of a scale until and unless money changed hands; any souvenir I bought would require a certificate declaring it was not an "antiquity." Hard currency legitimized all purchases. Those presenting airplane tickets at a check-in counter were informed their names weren't listed until the Queen's portrait appeared on banknotes. Every transaction had to be *fixed;* hence a *fixer*.

On arrival at Lagos, passengers stumbled between armed militia into a dimly lit hall and paraded before an interrogator glaring down from a high bench. A machine gun lay beside him. We shuffled slowly forward. The man before me in the queue was asked the purpose of his visit.

"Work," he explained.

"Where's your work permit?"

He had none. He was whisked from the line and disappeared. I heard no shots, but I'd learned a lesson. It was my turn to explain my presence.

"I'm here to consult."

"What will you consult?"

"It's confidential," I answered. I'd been well coached. Everything *confidential* carried a mysterious cachet. I went through.

I arrived in the state capital, Benin; my luggage didn't. I bought cloth at the local market and the local tailor, after several attempts, outfitted me. It would have been quicker had he taken my measurements. There was no urgency since I had nothing to do. No one knew anything about any Parliament. I passed my time with an engineer imported to carry out water studies that had already been done. We travelled about patronizing talented local artists and familiarizing ourselves with local construction resources. Local engineers were unreliable; forging university diplomas was a thriving industry. Few could read plans and fewer could implement them.

The town depended on an Israeli team operating systems that sporadically and unpredictably provided electricity and potable water that would be a bacteriologist's delight. The team was hidden in the bush because Nigeria, for reasons of high politics, didn't recognize Israel at that time; it probably lacked a *fixer*. But their ideals didn't extend to refusing or acknowledging assistance.

Construction materials consisted of home-made concrete blocks baked in the sun, asbestos-cement panels, metal formed sheets—and mud. The local variety was particularly cohesive and could readily be excavated and formed into the walls. When eroded by rain they were easily repaired by applying more mud. I mused that, had we used this material for our project, Parliament could have been dissolved by a fire hose.

There was ample wood in the jungle. It was cut and sawn, but mostly for export. The few carpenters that had been trained lacked expertise and materials for anything but the simplest construction. Any available concrete was of uncertain quality; cement that arrived by ship waited a year in the Lagos harbour to be unloaded. By that time it had hardened into concrete. A newly constructed cement plant was inoperative because the dust collectors, never having been emptied, had collapsed. Machines and equipment purchased through foreign aid lay unpacked in their boxes because there were no engineers to collect and assemble them. They were ransacked or left to rust.

Bureaucracy devised a task for me: a small twin-engine motor-boat would take me down the Niger River to the delta where drilling for oil had started. The Governor sought creative proposals to develop the territory. The trip took longer than expected because only one engine operated, allowing me to leisurely view a swampy sanctuary for snakes, crocodiles and every insect known to man, and for many unknown. It was hot and humid. Everything festered. Buildings that had served Nigeria's colonial past had rotted away.

My opinion on investment was solicited. I fought off the temptation to suggest that a spa for Weight Watchers would guarantee quick results for obese guests. The local population wouldn't need it; nobody was overweight.

I returned to my base and passed the time designing a badly needed public toilet. It required little imagination: concrete block walls on a concrete floor with openings properly sized and spaced. I'd come to Nigeria to design a Parliament and left having produced a public toilet. It seemed a microcosm of an architectural career: a descent from aspiration to realization; some might say "...to defecation."

It came time to return. Accompanied by my engineering confrère, I took my open ticket to Air Nigeria to be validated. The office was open, but empty. We returned the next day. And the day after. The office remained open but unoccupied. I feared we'd have to apply for Nigerian citizenship, but my engineer knew what to do: he completed our tickets with appropriate codes and threw in a night in a London hotel. At the airport our *fixer* crossed enough palms to ensure that we and the baggage were safely aboard, we parted with what remained of our worthless local currency, and we relaxed in contemplation of clean sheets and edible fare. The plane was hardly airborne when it was shaken by a loud bang—a tire had exploded and its shredded remains jammed the hydraulic system. We circled back, worried more about the prospect of re-entering and again departing from Nigeria, with its rapacious officials than about crash-landing on our undercarriage. The wheels came down and locked and I survived to write these memoirs.

Arriving in London, we made directly for the British Airways desk to confirm arrangements for our return. Naturally no record existed, but we had tickets and righteous indignation on our side. There was no further problem. We didn't even need our *fixer*.

...designing a bus terminal in thin Bolivian air

In 1979 I was invited by a prominent engineering company to design the central bus terminal in La Paz to serve as the hub for the entire country. It was Thursday; I'd have to leave the following Monday. I spoke no Spanish, the metric system that was the standard for most nations had yet not been adopted in Canada, and I'd never designed a bus terminal. I agreed immediately.

I made for the offices of the local Voyageur Bus Company and examined drawings of their terminals. Since they differed little in principle from airports I foresaw no design difficulties. The air in La Paz, what there was of it at about twelve thousand feet above sea level, was fresh, brisk, and almost free of oxygen. Fortunately my chronically sluggish metabolism accommodated itself and I continued to breathe. The engineer accompanying me was not as fortunate; he needed recourse to oxygen tanks that were found in every hotel room.

The site had not been selected; they looked to me to find a suitable venue in the sprawling city. After I consulted maps, traffic patterns, and access points, I found a suitable open space in central La Paz. The government intervened: the space was reserved for the Bolivian Navy Command.

"But Bolivia has no seacoast," I protested.

"True," came the answer. "We lost our access to the Pacific in a war with Chile a century ago, but we expect to re-conquer the territory."

They agreed to build the terminal on the naval property with the understanding it would be re-located after Bolivia's future victory. It seemed reasonable.

I found that Bolivia had many small bus lines with vehicles of every design, size, and condition. There was no central ticketing; some vehicles carried baggage on the roof, some between the wheels, some on racks, and the rest on top of the passengers. We made order out of chaos.

Life in La Paz was delightful. Meals consisted of meat, meat, and meat. Even the entertainment was beef: bullfights. I attended one. I was asked by the ticket seller where I wished to sit. I asked: "How high can a bull jump?" and took a seat several rows higher.

It was time for the yearly national parade. Every Bolivian village had spent twelve months since the last parade making more fantastic costumes and practicing more rhythmic dances attuned to drums and wind instruments fashioned from plants and trees. Wood benches lined the entire route. Several days before the parade was to start these were mostly filled with spectators. We reserved a couple of places and hired sitters to keep them until the festivities began. The parade was an indescribable feast for eyes and ears. We left after twelve hours, long before the last dancers had shown off their costumes and dancing skills and departed for their villages to prepare for next year's celebration.

After a delightful couple of months we left a group of happy Bolivians behind with our drawings. True to South America's tradition of mañana, they never built anything. But then, they never had their war either. It, too, was mañana.

...building an airport on sand

Abu Dhabi, a United Arab Emirate on the Persian Gulf, was then ruled by Sheikh Shakhbut Bin Sultan Al Nahyan. The country, largely desert only a few feet above sea level, was then emerging as a major oil producer.

Its neighbour, Dubai, already had an airport and a bridge; Abu Dhabi had neither. It was not to be borne; national pride was affronted. British engineers were hired to build these facilities. They found that the body of water to be crossed by a bridge was exceedingly shallow and recommended construction of a causeway. But a causeway is not a bridge and the British engineers were sent home. They were replaced by a consortium of Canadian engineering companies prepared to erect the spans without raising foolish objections. In 1966 I was invited to design the terminal buildings, a hotel, and the decorative features of the new bridge. There was a complication: obtaining a visa to the Sheikhdom required that I supply a birth certificate. We all agreed that such a document, prominently featuring the *mohel* who'd circumcised me, would raise political questions better left unasked. I joined with Tex Dawson, my former fellow student, an excellent architect and a certified gentile, to represent us. On his arrival in Abu Dhabi he was directed to an expatriate doctor for a cholera inoculation. He protested that he'd received his injection in Canada, but rules were rules. They had several drinks before the doctor scratched Tex's arm with an ointment. Infection set in; the limb turned black and complications threatened. Fortunately his arm was spared further sorrow but healing was very slow. I remained safely home and healthy, thanks to my circumcision.

The airport requirements were simple: Dubai's runway was nine thousand feet long; therefore Abu Dhabi's runway must stretch for ten thousand feet. Design of the terminal and a connecting hotel proceeded briskly; the only changes involved progressive enlargement of the reception hall until it occupied virtually the entire floor space, large enough to impress any visiting dignitary. Construction was uneventful and the result was so favourable it was featured on local postage stamps that I'm compelled to display to interested parties on a moment's notice.

Work progress and newsworthy events at the site were reported on tapes we received weekly. They related how the throne of Sheikh Shakhbut Bin Sultan Al Nahyan was lifted onto an aircraft with the Sheikh seated on it and flown to London at the instigation of his brother, Sheikh Zaid Bin Sultan Al Nahayan, whose desire for power exceeded his filial devotion. Possibly Canadians can profit from this innovative way of changing the government without the useless expense of an election.

We also learned that the Sheikh, who disdained banknotes in favour of gold in payment for oil, was missing a million pounds worth of his precious bars from under his bed. He convoked his wise men. They conferred and recommended that everyone in the palace be fed olives in the expectation that the guilty party would choke on a pit. I didn't hear the end of the story, but neither did I forget it. I've kept unpitted olives at home ever since. One never knows.

Our presence in Abu Dhabi led to proposals for other projects. An Egyptian prince asked for a quotation on a palace that would have more bedrooms than an average hotel, seat more than a hundred guests for banquets, and require a kitchen large enough to roast a whole camel and a hundred sheep. Our estimator couldn't find information on camel roasters and nothing came of it.

A more serious proposal was solicited for two prisons, one for each local sub-Sheikh. I consulted Canadian penologists and submitted a list of questions relevant to prison design: Number, age and gender of prisoners? Length of sentences? Guidelines for parole and rehabilitation? Visitation rights and conjugal visits? Prison activities? Current prison practices and experience? Segregation of disturbed or dangerous inmates?

The answer was quick and simple: Each Sheikh has his own prisoners locked in iron cages in the walled courtyard of his palace where he can count them every day. The rest of the questions didn't merit answers.

... adventures in the Canadian Arctic

My Arabian desert experience contrasted sharply with my work in the Canada's north, principally the region inhabited by ten Cree villages. A thousand kilometers north of Montreal six of Quebec's largest rivers empty into James Bay, providing immense potential for hydroelectric development. In the 1970s the main tributary, La Grande Rivière, was being dammed to flood almost ten thousand square kilometers. By 1980 the village at the mouth of the river, Fort George, with its two thousand inhabitants, would be relocated and transformed into a major village, Chisasibi. This project, and its spin-offs, occupied me for five years.

Some houses of the original village were jacked from their foundations, transported four miles upstream over difficult terrain, and renovated to modern standards. But most of the homes would be new and their design would be governed by native culture and lifestyle; construction materials and techniques would be compatible with climate, local construction skills, and logistic limitations.

Eventually we became responsible for housing and for many public buildings in all the Cree communities.

I quickly discovered that earlier houses supplied by the government were inadequate: insulation was insufficient, vapour and air barriers were ineffective, energy conservation hadn't been considered, condensation degraded walls and roofs, and mould proliferated in the damp dwellings. No thought had been given to native lifestyle and occupants hadn't been instructed on maintenance procedures that promoted health, comfort, and building integrity. There was much to do and it involved ongoing dialogue with the population. We all learned from the process.

But such consultation had its own imperatives. Everyone in each village followed the design process assiduously. Chiefs did not make decisions: these required unanimous tribal consent that was only achieved after endless public meetings and intense politicking. It was not a quick process; I had a lot of learning, listening, and persuading to do.

The local population understood plans and were skillful and conscientious builders, except when ducks or geese flew overhead. Then they all dropped their tools and started shooting, a right that was enshrined in their contracts. During those seasons they enjoyed nothing more than rising before dawn, lying in a marsh, and peppering those birds. They'd gleefully bring their bloody carcasses home, happily exchanging tales of their prowess. It was their way of life; they'd survived by hunting, fishing, and trapping for thousands of years; it was in their blood. To the detriment of native life and culture these skills are disappearing, leaving social problems in their wake. These are compounded by pollution that impacts inhabitants and wildlife.

I had to deal with -40° temperatures, blinding snow storms, short winter days, and paucity of local resources. Transportation facilities were primitive; no roads connected the settlements except when the ground and waterways froze solidly enough to support truck traffic. As "summer" approached, vehicles crossing lakes kept anxious eyes on the ice. They drove with their doors open to facilitate a quick exit—and such an exit was essential. The first truck that plunged through the ice signalled the end of winter transport. It was a quick and sure way, albeit expensive, of determining the road's useful life.

Materials and equipment that could be sent by boat during short shipping seasons had to be securely packaged. Cargoes were dropped onto barges, dumped onto beaches, and dragged to building sites. The only other freight access was by planes capable of carrying limited loads and able to land on primitive strips, unassisted by navigation aids and subjected to unpredictable and highly variable weather. Passenger air traffic between villages and southern towns was by small, propeller-driven aircraft, also dependent on vagaries of weather and risks of visual approaches. Flight rules were lax: hand luggage might consist of a washing machine, or half a butchered caribou. Loading was informal: baggage was piled into the rear compartment until the nose wheel tilted off the ground. Then we took off.

The challenges were exhilarating. Major engineering companies were employed and I worked closely with their talented personnel. Among them was Einar Skinnarland, a Norwegian familiar with construction in remote, cold areas. His appearance was unremarkable: medium height, slightly rotund, with a pleasant, demeanor. He was an agreeable companion and a good friend. A fellow engineer asked me: "Did I realize who Skinnarland was?" I pleaded ignorance. I learned that my mild, modest, friendly Skinnarland had been a key figure in terminating German efforts during the Second World War to create what we now call "weapons of mass destruction."

The Norsk Hydro plant at Vermork, Norway, was the only facility in Europe that produced heavy water needed to process plutonium. After German forces occupied that country in 1940, British intelligence learned that production would be greatly increased. Disturbed by this report, they parachuted commandos into Norway to destroy the facility. The commandos were readily recognized, caught, tortured, and executed. The Germans were thereby alerted that the plant had become a target. The job needed local talent able to survive in the mountains and mount an effective raid.

Skinnarland, then a young Norwegian hydroelectrical technician, was part of a group that hijacked a small ship and diverted it to Scotland. In a few days of intensive training he learned how to operate a radio, jump from a plane, and sabotage an industrial facility. Dropped into the Norwegian wilderness, he made his way to the tightly guarded Norsk Hydro plant where his technical education gained him employment. He was now able to report on security measures and guide a team of Norwegian commandos into the facility where their explosives ended any possibility of heavy water production.

Skinnarland then reported to London via his clandestine radio that the entire remaining stock, fourteen tonnes of heavy water, would be shipped to German researchers. This information led the saboteurs to attach explosives to the keel of the vessel and sink the vessel with its cargo, thereby thwarting any further enemy progress in this field. These exploits are celebrated in the film *The Heroes of Telemark*; Skinnarland was one of those heroes.

In the months that Skinnarland and I worked together, he never mentioned his dangerous activities. That was my only brush with history; having little courage myself, I unstintingly admired those who possessed it

Expanding on our experience in Cree communities, we ventured another one thousand kilometers north to Inuit villages. These lined Quebec's north coast, where the shipping season was even shorter, the temperatures even lower, and winds, unimpeded by forests, froze unprotected skin in seconds. Anyone foolhardy enough to venture outside could be blinded by wind-driven snow, become confused, and wander off, never to be found until the summer thaw. Ropes were attached from building to building to provide safe passage during these storms.

Buildings were erected on permanently frozen ground (permafrost), often hundreds of feet deep. They were designed to prevent the soil under the foundations from liquefying. I write of conditions that prevailed several decades ago; recent warming trends will result in important changes to architecture, villagers' economy, and community lifestyle.

Lands of the high Arctic, although usually snow-covered, had little precipitation. What water existed was usually insufficient for fire protection. Surface water was frozen most of the year and wells were unknown. Because many building materials were combustible, any blaze gaining a foothold could not be extinguished. Larger structures required extraordinary measures: for example, major elements of a school would be divided into wings (classrooms, gymnasium, library, and offices) all connected by passageways. If a fire started in one section its connecting passageway would be quickly bulldozed to control flame spread. Unique construction was developed to cope with problems not known in temperate zones. I completed several schools and community buildings, struggling to marry southern technology with northern lifestyle, as expressed through their native language, Inuktitut.

... dealing with a blasted building

A large chemical company close to Montreal had built a facility to produce sodium azide, a chemical found in every car fitted with airbags. When a vehicle suddenly stops, as in a collision, the chemical is triggered and the explosion inflates the airbag. The company had undertaken to supply a major car manufacturer with this material. Failure to deliver on an agreed schedule would result in a penalty of fifty thousand dollars a day.

A process building was erected in 1990, and within weeks of the start of production an explosion killed several workers and heavily damaged the facility. I was mandated to determine the cause of the accident and propose measures to re-start manufacturing with minimum delay. Making a quick study of the characteristics of sodium azide I prepared to inspect the premises.

"Do you have high blood pressure?" I was asked. "Exposure to this dust can be fatal."

My blood pressure was low, at least until I heard this warning.

"Well, take no chances. Don't lick your lips while inside." I agreed.

"And wear metal-soled boots to avoid sparking while you walk. Do your feet conduct electricity efficiently?"

"I haven't visited my electrician recently." They tested my feet.

"They're too dry. You must wear wet socks."

That was how I came to slosh around a wrecked explosives plant in steel-soled shoes, remembering not to lick my lips.

I found that the plant had transgressed all the rules for producing this unstable substance. It needed to be demolished, redesigned, and re-built. Other experts were consulted; all agreed. Mindful of impending penalties, the company ordered us to proceed at top speed.

We mobilized: our personnel slaved twenty-four hours a day, seven days a week, to design the facility, barely keeping ahead of building crews who also laboured night and day. Drawings flew off our boards; construction phases followed seamlessly. Everyone worked frantically—except the local building permit officials. They strolled to work as usual. For them there was no urgency, no pressure, no penalty clause—it was business as usual. They unrolled drawings, sipped coffee, and questioned work that had long been completed. There are always questions, especially in a specialized plant producing hazardous materials. On some issues involving delicate production operations where timely decisions could not be made, we polled the employees to obtain their approval.

For example: the most dangerous part of the process involved mixing unstable elements to produce sodium azide. This operation was carried out in a series of rooms only large enough to contain the operator and necessary mixers; each space was no larger than a bathroom. The Building Code required two exits from any hazardous area; there was barely space for one. The bureaucrat in charge of our file demanded a second door. I explained that there was no risk of fire, only of explosion. In this event the sole occupant of his tiny enclosure would have little time to decide which door to use—he'd either be blown through the wall or through the roof. This and countless other issues were discussed at length while construction proceeded non-stop.

Somehow, I survived, although I often came close to exploding myself. No one asked me for my blood pressure; I was content not to know.

... lost in Newfoundland

Visiting far-off projects brought me my share of thrills, some with a humourous side.

In 1962 I designed a housing project in Baie Verte, Newfoundland. After the first winter the roofs leaked, and I was sent to investigate. I flew to Gander, landing in a dense fog; further travel was impossible until it would clear. While waiting in the airport I bought the largest lobster I could find for my daughter: a bright red fabric shell with fearsome claws, all stuffed with sponge. The fog refused to lift. After several days being paid to sit on an airport bench clutching my oversized crustacean, the pilot decided: "Well, m'boy, let's try it."

I didn't like the sound of it, but business was business. The two of us crowded into the cockpit of his small amphibian plane. "Here, m'boy, you navigate," he said, and thrust a map purchased from a gas station at me. He needn't have bothered. We couldn't see the propeller of our plane as we wavered through the gray clouds that blanketed the region.

"Well, m'boy," my pilot reflected. "The sea's somewhere here. I'm goin' down. Usually they's clear air just over the water and we'll find ourselves a fishing village. Somewhere." And we did. He set the plane down guided it across the waves to the fishing dock. It was crowded with villagers; they don't have a plane visiting every day. They lifted me onto the pier, paying special attention to my stuffed lobster. I was the catch of the day. The pilot stayed on with his amphibian and I completed the trip seated in a taxi accompanied by that lobster.

Oh, yes—the roofs leaked because the edges of the shingles lifted in the high coastal winds. But they solved that problem. They had nailed those shingles down real tight, each and every one of them.

Winding up

I ask my readers: what profession could be more exciting, or interesting, or satisfying? Certainly not selling sundries and smallware, even those starting with an A. Not all projects were unusual or adventurous, but each was at least a little different and many presented unique challenges. And I never lost an eye—although, on several occasions, I was concerned that Ma's prophecies might be fulfilled.

Considering my many years of travel, the diversity of my pilots, chauffeurs, and guides, and the variety and questionable quality of their vehicles to which I entrusted my life, I was lucky to have emerged unscathed. My closest brush with the hereafter occurred at London's Heathrow Airport in 1986: as I queued for a final hand luggage inspection preparatory to boarding an aircraft destined for Israel, a young lady preceding me was pulled from the line. Security police flourishing machine guns immediately circled us, we were herded to the centre of the terminal, all planes were towed to the ends of the runways, and we waited.... and waited. Several hours later we were driven to our planes, searched again and sniffed by dogs; they turned up their noses and we boarded. I learned that our lady traveller carried a bag with a false bottom hiding a bomb timed to explode over Europe. It was a gift from an Arab lover who promised to marry her in Israel; she was pregnant, and ignorant of his plan to terminate their relationship along with the lives of four hundred passengers. Her fiancé was arrested in London; I presume that the nuptials were delayed.

Despite enjoying the hospitality of many countries with dubious culinary reputations, I was spared when my travelling companions retched from air/sea sickness or food poisoning, or were felled by fevers, scorpions, dog bites, or other foreign specialties. Excepting my bout with polio in Israel, I remained intact. Back home, thanks to Ma's nutrition and her timely cautionary advice, I was healthy throughout my productive years in a profession where stamina was a necessity.

★ ★ ★

It's been a wonderful life. I encountered diverse cultures, political systems, and social mores, and realized that human folly, greed, and lust for power are universal; pockets of love, kindness, and mercy are few and feeble. Whenever I returned from working in continents rife with poverty and oppression, I blessed my country— there are few like it. I learned what was wrong with the world, but not how to fix it. Anyone seeking guidance or counselling is welcome to visit me; I'm always ready to advise about what I know—

or don't. I may not have good advice, but I have lots of good stories.

I still continue a modest consulting practice from my home office, assisted by my computer, Internet, email, and other marvels of communication. It's work I enjoy. I learn from every case.

Playing the expert allows me to sit with a solemn and knowing expression on a face wrinkled with memories of almost sixty years of tiptoeing through minefields of design and construction. Happily none of the mines exploded—yet. I write wise reports calling attention to errors and omissions for design professionals, builders, lawyers, insurers, and claimants in legal proceedings. They profit from my years of angst. Presiding judges look at my remaining white hairs and conclude I must have learned something. I did: I know several thousand things that don't work. It's priceless information that took a lifetime to acquire. I can't predict my final destination, but if my services are required in either heaven or hell I'm ready to serve either God or the Devil—my decades of experience must count for something.

★ ★ ★

This part of the Memoir would not be complete without acknowledging the contribution of those who worked with and for me. We all understood the rules of the game: an architectural practice reeks with uncertainty. Revenue slows when projects are scarce and halts when they disappear. Completed work must be replaced; no practice can survive a long drought and valued workers must be laid off during prolonged slack periods, and, if available, rehired when conditions change. Discharging personnel was a dreadful duty, and, as a practicing coward, I delegated this distasteful duty to other partners.

When computers replaced pencils, many old-time architects and technicians couldn't adapt, and had to be replaced. There were few jobs for them and they became victims of a new industrial revolution. By this time, I was engaged in soliciting new work, administering our office and in overseeing major projects. None of these duties required advanced computer skills—my calligraphic talents, my well-honed drafting abilities all became worthless. This was the cost of progress. It was bitter price for many.

I'm proud that we developed a well-run team, and that so many enjoyed lengthy careers with us. They made it all possible.

PART 2

...AND THOSE WHO ENRICHED MY YEARS

PEOPLE IN MY LIFE

My life, orbiting around Ma and Pa, was also influenced by a constellation of relatives and friends who twinkled in other nebulae—more distant, but still subject to our family's gravity. There were many who deserved mention, and I regret that this Memoir couldn't include more of these worthy souls.

Sidney, Sol, and Harold: the Moon Brothers

Sidney, Sol, and Harold were my mother's brothers. In keeping with our family's nonchalant attitude to chronology, exact birth dates are, and will forever remain, uncertain; they were not recorded, disclosed, discussed, or celebrated. Families were large to compensate for high infant mortality and the arrival of a new baby was associated with an event: a barn burning, a pogrom, an epidemic, or any convenient catastrophe. The day, month, and year were immaterial. This vagueness raised questions in their adopted country, as contradictory anniversaries were entered at random whenever required by official forms. No one knew for sure, nor cared; one guess was as good as another. People lived, worked, and prospered. That was important.

Ma's oldest sibling was Harold, the youngest, Sidney. Sol was sandwiched somewhere between them. They were known collectively as the Moon Brothers because, between them, they had no more hair than the lunar landscape. Our genetic inheritance featured early, intractable, and irreversible loss of scalp cover. Only Sidney carefully nursed a few pathetic threads that he guided across his shining pate and fastened by spit; he was known as The Importer, because he brought strands over from the other side. The females

Many members of the family. Back row, l. to r., the Moon brothers, Sol and Harold Ivry, My Pa Harry Reich, Uncle Nathan Reich, Moe Blostein and Moon brother Sidney Ivry. Front row, Aunts Sochie (Ivry) Rabin, Rose (Brull) Ivry, Annie (Corman) Ivry, Miriam (Ivry) Reich, Billie Ivry of New York, and Lisl (Epstein) Ivry, circa 1955.

had some hair, but *luxurious* did not come to mind: they had to work to make it known, artfully combing it to disguise the sparse roots from which it had sprung. It was a barren harvest.

My three uncles looked startlingly alike. They were short, oval, with small bulbous noses and, of course, completely hairless above their eyebrows.

Sidney, the most animated, gregarious, and voluble, was a salesman. He told stories, tickled a piano keyboard by ear and drove a car expertly; he was a social creature, a friend to all.

Harold was immersed in music and wrote poetry in Yiddish. Aside from reciting his rhymes, he spoke little, probably because he popped grapes into his mouth with one hand and spat the seedlings into the other: pht, pht, pht..... with the staccato rapidity of a machine gun. Professionally, he was a violinist: not of international renown, but talented enough to play in clubs and at celebrations. His modest career terminated when Ma informed him that his future lay in The Store. Late in life he married Annie who became the champion he needed.

Sol talked even less; he usually sat smiling to himself as he peeled small, seedless green grapes and thoughtfully chewed them. His career included peddling from door to door principally in Chinatown, and he counted in Chinese to entertain me. Our conversations never went deeper. He couldn't drive, but he did, as will be described later. Sol was a bachelor of long standing, but he eventually succumbed to Rose. She spoke for him; any question addressed to Sol was answered by her.

"Would you like a potato, Sol?"

"A small one," she would respond.

Naturally she was known to the family as The Ventriloquist. They were childless. It was probably just another topic they never discussed.

Clearly the Moon Brothers were not the decision makers within the family. Ma was the unquestioned directress of her siblings and of everyone else related by blood or marriage. Her force of gravity equalled that of any black hole in the universe. When not contradicted, she was benevolent, dispensing warmth, wisdom, and direction. We could conceive of no other world.

All the Moon Brothers were eventually sucked into Reich Brothers Limited; The Store flourished and expanded, chiefly by absorbing newly arrived relatives, until at least ten of our families were supported by sundries, novelties, and smallware it imported. I was a notable exception, but my brother, uncles, cousins, and related folk were conscripted. Ma explained to the recruits what was best for them. They understood, and in most cases, the arrangement was satisfactory. Their options were limited.

The Moon Brothers adapted themselves to their new country.

★ ★ ★

Harold loved music. In Lithuania, he had been directed to a medical career but his studies in Konigsberg, Prussia, were interrupted by the First World War. He returned home to be considered a German spy and was tied to a tree to await execution. How he escaped is not known, but it was said he was never the same. He lost any medical ambitions he had and returned to his first love—the violin—it was less risky. When not practicing Bach, Beethoven, or Brahms, he immersed himself in his poetry. That was his life.

His poetic talent was displayed at *kultur abends* regularly held in my parents' living room on Saturday nights, the only time of week when anyone, except the cleaning lady, was admitted into this sacrosanct space. Ma's soirées, described earlier, were attended by her friends, mostly of Russian origin; they were emotional, loving, and filled with a love of drama inherited from dark Slavic novels and plays. I was expected to greet them as they entered. I didn't mind shaking hands with their husbands, but kissing the powdered and rouged cheeks of middle-aged would-be ingénues was disconcerting. They were a happy group, chattering away in many languages and increasingly in heavily accented English. All met my mother's strict criteria for respectability, gentility, and character.

Midway through these evenings, before serving tea to wash down cakes and cookies that preserved our guests' generous figures, Harold would come to life and fumble through his pockets.

"I've written something, I have it here, somewhere, I'm sure, something, somewhere," he would mutter to himself in Yiddish, just loud enough for all to hear.

As expected, he produced his sheaf of papers covered with Yiddish script that he proceeded to read to the assembly until his wife forcefully intervened: "Hershel, genig!" ("Harold, enough!")—otherwise he might have recited until dawn. After each stanza, he looked meaningfully at his audience to make sure that they understood the subtleties of his rhymes. Ma had the same talent, and my literary career, using the term loosely, undoubtedly sprang from Ivry genes, even to the meaningful looks.

Harold's irregular hours in the music trade had kept him occupied all night and asleep all day, a habit that he cultivated into a life-long addiction. During an extended bachelorhood, he shared a modest apartment with Sidney, Sol, and his brother-in-law, Moe Blostein. The rooms were perpetually darkened to suit this nocturnal schedule. During the day, a ghostly yellow light filtered through the blinds, casting eerie shadows of mounds of sheet music that reached almost to the ceiling. A few pieces of furniture loomed out of this unrelieved dusk. I wouldn't have been surprised to see bats flitting about. Every Sunday morning I visited their dim lodgings and was rewarded by a dime that would last me a whole week.

When Harold traded his violin for Reich Brothers' order forms, it became apparent that he was especially unsuited to business. The sleeping routine he faithfully maintained did not add to his effectiveness. He had a tendency to doze on any of the shelves lining the recesses of the warehouse to which he had been condemned; he became part of the inventory. Once he awoke to find himself locked in The Store after closing. His absence was eventually noted and he had to be rescued in the dead of night because the burglar alarm had been set and the telephone de-activated. No one was surprised. He had often fallen asleep on ladders and shelves. Sustained consciousness during conventional working hours was not among his assets.

Harold had a gift for such mishaps. The Store had a dumbwaiter to handle small quantities of merchandise. A bell would alert any worker on the floor where the lift was parked to send it to another destination. Harold rang the bell. The dumbwaiter did not appear. Several rings followed with no reaction. It struck Harold that the dumbwaiter might be lost and struck him even more forcibly when it hit his head as he looked up the shaft. He recovered, scarred, but still able to sleep.

Harold, in his artistic innocence, espoused harmless and naive socialist philosophies. My father, a dedicated anti-Communist and a man of simple, direct and rigid principles, seldom referred to him favourably. To be a musician incapable of making a secure livelihood was bad enough, but to be a communist to boot—well there were limits! And daytime slumber was an aberration he could never accept, although he managed to forgive himself for his own naps. He had earned them.

After a prolonged unattached existence Harold married Annie. Her respect, support, and appreciation of his music and poetry compensated to some extent for his lack of stature in family councils. Undistracted by offspring, Harold fiddled away his retirement from Reich Brothers' shelves in quiet contentment, living to an advanced age that, like the longevity of many Ivry family members, would never exactly be determined.

Ma's passing, although sad, had some light moments because of Harold. Lionel and I divided the formalities attending Ma's decease: I undertook to complete the forms required by the authorities and Lionel busied himself ordering the tombstone to be undraped at the graveside unveiling ceremony. I visited the government offices, met *Fonctionnaire X*, received the appropriate forms and did my best to fill in the blanks. When I came to *Date de Naissance*; my conversation with *Fonctionnaire X* went something like this:

"Monsieur X, we don't know my mother's date of birth."

"Monsieur Reich, you have only to look at her certificate of birth."

"Alas, Monsieur X, Madame Reich has no certificate of birth."

The good *Monsieur X* had difficulty understanding the absence of this document. In Quebec society every infant had a baptismal record or its equivalent, duly registered in Church records that had been meticulously maintained since the first settlers had landed in what was New France four hundred years earlier.

"But Monsieur Reich, the blank must be filled. Obtain this certificate from her town."

"*Monsieur X*, the town is in Lithuania. It has been devastated by wars. Dates of birth, especially of females, were of no importance and seldom registered."

"Monsieur Reich, the blank exists. It must be filled. Otherwise the good Madame never officially died. Did she not complete any forms while she lived in Canada?"

Ma had more than her share of hospital admissions, insurance applications, and memberships; she'd dutifully given her date of birth a number of times—each one had been different. Ma never bothered to remember what she'd written before. What difference did it make? I explained this.

"Monsieur Reich, something must be done. A blank blank is impermissible."

An idea crossed my mind. "Her older brother still lives. Would a sworn affidavit from Harold Ivry be acceptable?"

"Mais oui, Monsieur Reich!"

I selected one of the dates Ma had used, prepared the affidavit and took it to Harold. He refused to sign. He didn't remember when she'd been born and if he perjured himself he risked deportation.

"Harold, Ma was over seventy-five; no one knows when she was born. One date is as good as another and there's no one alive to contradict you."

He was adamant. In such cases there's always a sure recourse. I turned to his wife. She understood.

"Hershel, shreib!" ("Harold, sign!") she commanded; the voice brooked no contradiction. He signed.

Meanwhile Lionel had ordered a tombstone. We'd never consulted on what birth date to use and he'd selected one at random.

The family attended the unveiling. The rabbi intoned the melancholy benedictions, the cloth fell away from the stone and the Ma's date of birth, chiselled in granite, lay exposed: it differed from that on Harold's affidavit. His misinformation was permanently set in granite. He worried about it for the rest of his days but successfully avoided deportation.

Sadly, he did not long survive Ma. His estate consisted of several violins, countless sheets of music and, of course: his Yiddish poems. Harold's poetry had more merit than we had appreciated, and at Annie's instigation, the family privately published his literary output. The volume now dozes as comfortably on the shelves of the National Jewish Book Centre as its author did on the shelves of The Store.

★ ★ ★

Sidney was a teenager when he arrived in Montreal. Before he was conscripted into The Store, he was a "sitter." It was a profession that required little training. There were many restaurants and passersby were loath to enter an empty one—obviously customers avoided the place for good reason. Therefore any establishment opening its doors for the first time needed live people to sit around tables pretending to enjoy meals. And if they had no customers, they hired "sitters"; the pay was small but the coffee was free.

If Harold was obsessed by music, Sidney was engrossed by postage stamps. His collection was sizable and its value great. He hobnobbed with similarly dedicated philatelists and he was proud to show me catalogues and display esoteric specialties he had assembled. Being more active and vocal than his brothers, he was appointed sales manager. As such, he collected buyers with the same intensity that he collected his stamps. He constantly referred to his good friends: John, buyer for Eaton's, Reggie, buyer for Morgan's, and so on. Their business cards, their Christmas cards, and other memorabilia covered his desk.

He was the first Moon Brother to marry. Gertie Shuchat was an amiable lady, but died suddenly while quite young, before she became part of our lives. Sidney re-married. This was frowned upon. I had the distinct impression that the Deity, personified by Ma, disapproved of second mates: her sister, Miriam Reich, her brother-in-law, Moe Blostein, her niece, Esther Rabin, all having lost spouses early in life, were only entitled to one ride on the merry-go-round.

Sidney's new bride, Lisl, younger than he, was a Holocaust survivor of Czech origin. Her story is told later. When it appeared she could bear no children, they adopted little Elsa. Shortly after, Lisl conceived and gave birth to Victor.

They lived in a Montreal suburb, Côte Saint-Luc, that, despite its identification with a saint, was, and remains predominantly inhabited by Jews. Quebec had not evolved to the point where towns were named after rabbis, no matter how holy. The population was well served by an abundance of synagogues and parochial schools at different levels of religious intensity. Scholastic and artistic excellence were prized as passports to achievement.

Jewish clubs, social organizations, and services for all ages flourished. Families competed to provide lessons of every sort to improve their children. Recalcitrant offspring were delivered by the busload to instructors of ballet, piano, voice—any skill recognized to promote family social standing and distinction.

Both of Sidney's children were brought up in this milieu. Jewish learning, tradition, and personal achievement stuck to Elsa like peas to a Teflon ceiling. Victor, on the other hand, was an achiever. An excellent swimmer of Olympic quality, he matched scholarship with unerring business sense. Eventually he settled in San Francisco, nurtured a profitable enterprise and raised three daughters in the best Jewish tradition. Elsa chose a different path: at her earliest opportunity she married a gentile in church on *Yom Kippur*, the holiest day of the Jewish calendar, begat two daughters, divorced, and is employed as a medical secretary. We seldom see her.

Through all this, Sidney remained a collector. Nothing was thrown out. While he was sales manager at The Store he had a mild heart attack. While he recuperated, his office desk was excavated from under a thick stratum of documents, an archeological site dating back to the first day of his occupancy. Not a letter, note, or Christmas card had ever been discarded.

Stamps did not fully satisfy his collecting mania and he soon had an outstanding assortment of spoons, coins, and medals. He died in the late 1980s, leaving a basement full of these treasures that are, to this day, being sold off by Lisl.

$$\star\ \star\ \star$$

Sol was the most reclusive and silent of the Moon Brothers. He remained a bachelor until middle age and then, to everyone's great surprise, appeared with an intended bride. Rose Brull was a piano teacher and, although pleasant and innocuous, never competed with Miss America. They were childless. As mentioned, Sol didn't communicate with anyone and, as we discovered, that included his wife. He died, probably too busy peeling his grapes to disclose the location of his bank accounts or securities that kept turning up, according to family lore, hidden among his underwear or under a car seat. I have no personal knowledge of this, but that it could be believed is testimony to his taciturn nature.

Sidney could drive a car. Harold never sat behind a wheel.

But Sol drove, giving new meaning to the word. In today's world he never would have been accorded a driver's license, but his car was one of a small fleet of vehicles that belonged to The Store, and could legally, if not safely, be driven by family members. In that simpler world driving tests were not required—prayers were. Sol was at a disadvantage when driving a vehicle, any vehicle, but especially one with a motor. He was uncoordinated and had absolutely no understanding of mechanical functioning of anything more complicated than a toothpick. His learning curve was dead flat. He vaguely understood that gasoline was involved. Beyond that, the display of dials, signals, and switches on the dashboard might have been decoration.

Early in his apprenticeship, I watched Sol as he slowly inched away from the curb, wavered uncertainly around the block to my Uncle Marcus' house, crossed his lawn, and wrapped the vehicle around a tree. The resounding crash brought everyone to their windows, to see Sol gazing in bewilderment at the smoking wreck. Another time I saw him enter The Store carrying the car bumper. "It fell off," he explained.

Cars in those days were far from automatic. Their gears were controlled by a floor-mounted stick that could be pushed in many directions if a clutch pedal was depressed. There were additional pedals for the brake and gas—three pedals for two feet—while one hand was on the wheel and a second on the gear stick. Traffic in Montreal depended on a talented cadre of traffic cops who pirouetted and gyrated at busy intersections, gracefully directing autos with flourishes worthy of skilled magicians or Indian dancers. Drivers would choose routes to see their favourites perform.

Once, Sol's car was signalled to halt at the top of a steep downtown street he was climbing. He remembered to step on the brake, depress the clutch, shift to neutral, all without stalling; he stopped, the first of a long line of cars following behind. After a decent interval, another flashing series of gestures motioned Sol to proceed. As Sol mentally reviewed the necessary procedures: shifting, clutching, unbraking, accelerating—the car rolled backwards, hammering the vehicle behind several feet down the slope. Sol braked and repeated the sequence. Another roll, another hammer blow. He pounded his hapless victim clear down to the bottom of the hill. Sol never learned. And, unbelievably, he died of natural causes: the family *freg nisht*.

Harold, Sidney, and Sol were good, ordinary people, loving and gentle, not unusually gifted or foolishly ambitious. They never did anyone harm and I remember with gratitude the dime they always gave me when I visited their gloomy apartment on Sunday morning. Its face value was ten cents, but it was worth a fortune.

These were Ma's younger brothers and she shaped their lives. She recognized their weaknesses, watched over them like a mother hen, and saw that they were gainfully employed in The Store. Like the rest of us, they had depended on her strength. We were family. They lived long lives and have now passed on.

I can see them in Paradise: Sidney is trading stamps, spoons, or medals with other departed collectors. Harold, when not chewing grapes and spitting out the seeds, is playing his violin and reciting his verses to the Almighty who doesn't miss a single Yiddish nuance; He speaks it as well as His native Hebrew. And Sol? He sits silently on a cloud, peeling grapes; they are seedless. He doesn't have to say anything; Rose is now with him. But he'll never get his wings. He couldn't pass the test.

The Rabins' Adventures in the Liver Trade

During the First World War, the German occupation of Vilkaviskis had not been oppressive; in fact, soldiers were billeted in the Ivry home. One of them, a Jewish officer, was attracted to Ma's maiden sister, Sochie, and the feeling was reciprocated. But first a war had to be settled. In 1917 the Bolshevik revolution shook Russia; when hostilities ended the German soldiers returned to their homeland. Sochie heard nothing from her suitor and soon found another, Yosef Rabin. The German-Jewish officer re-surfaced, but too late. Sochie had married and given birth to Esther and David. Hearts were broken and nerves were shattered, but, as usually happens, they mended. It was another example of how capricious actions of mighty rulers affect the lives of their subjects.

Yosef Rabin came to Canada in 1927 and settled in Ottawa. In 1929 Sochie joined him with her two babes, Esther and David. The air in our capital must have been brisk, as she bore two more boys in quick succession, Lionel and Eli.

To a newcomer, Ottawa was cold meteorologically, economically, and socially, and not especially hospitable to those outside its single industry: government. Yosef, with his imposing figure, impressive personality, musical ability, and quick wit, was extraordinarily multi-talented and soon became the chief purveyor of

Ma's family, the Ivrys in Vilkaviskis, Lithuania, circa 1919. Bottom, l. to r.,
Uncle Sidney Ivry and Aunt Miriam Ivry (100 years old in 2011). Middle,
My Ma, Jennie Ivry; my great grandmother, Esther Yavorovitz; my grandmother Chaya Tzipporah (Yavorovitz) Ivry; and my uncle Harold Ivry, Ma's
oldest brother. Top, Uncle Sol Ivry, Aunts Sochie and Leah Ivry.

services to the small Jewish community. He circumcised the new-
born as the *mohel*, he ritually slaughtered cattle and fowl as the *sho-
chet*, he led the congregation as *chazzin* in prayers, he trained the
choir, he taught *Torah* to Ottawa's junior Jews, and produced musical
compositions and arrangements that now repose in Archives
Canada. He was the Jewish Pooh-Bah. His fame spread and soon
he was putting the brand of Abraham on Jewish babies in remote
communities in northern Ontario, making his rounds by airplane
as The Flying Mohel. He became such a respected and indispensable part of the community that when he died many venerable years
later his funeral cortege through the streets of Canada's capital was
escorted by the city police through re-directed traffic.

Despite the scope of his activities and the vigour with which
Yosef pursued them, they were not wealthy. The small Ottawa Jewish
community could pay only a modest salary and money was always
short in the Rabin household, especially while educating one son

Yosef Rabin, aka The Flying Mohel, purveyed services to
Ottawa's small Jewish community.

Ma's sister Sochie Rabin and her husband Yosef Rabin of Ottawa supplied our
family and many others with Kosher liver.

to become an engineer and two others to become doctors. Indeed, he was often reimbursed with livers of cows he slaughtered; there's no record of his compensation for circumcisions. Liver was understandably a large part of our family diet and whenever Sochie came to Montreal to visit her brothers and sisters, she invariably carried a large and bloody beef liver wrapped in wax paper and the *Ottawa Citizen*. Sochie and liver were virtually Siamese twins and her visits to our home were always followed by weeks of chopped liver, fried liver, sautéd liver, and liver *kreplach*.

Inter-city travel was by train. Airplanes, except for daredevil circumcisers, hardly existed as public transportation. Immigrants were not used to busses that had indecipherable schedules that necessitated questioning non-Yiddish-speaking officials. Cars, when not used for delivering parcels, were for urban transport and for driving the children to the *contree* on Sunday, where they glimpsed mountains, trees, and even lakes.

When Sochie was due at Montreal's Windsor Station (later replaced by Central Station), one of the family was delegated to fetch her and her invariable travelling companion, the omnipresent oozing liver. It goes without saying that she was to be retrieved by a family member driving a family car. For us, taxis did not exist; they were considered profligacy of the worst sort. The thought of being taken by a driver of unproven competence in a strange vehicle while a meter remorselessly subtracted pennies from the family exchequer was unthinkable, almost irreligious. It fell into the same category as long distance phone calls and telegrams, to be used only on occasions involving life and death—nothing in between.

Only once did a communications failure between my brother, father, and myself leave Sochie stranded at the station with her liver-laden lap. My memory has blanked out how long she sat; it might have been for the entire weekend. The consequences to both Sochie and her cargo of liver were not recorded.

As Sochie and family arrived in Canada some ten years after my parents, their use of Yiddish persisted much longer than did ours. In fact, it never disappeared and I spent many delicious hours listening to their singsong banter as questions were answered by questions, all filled with rich metaphors and similes.

I spent one magic summer with the Rabin household in Ottawa while I worked as an architectural draftsman with a Crown corporation. Away from the close supervision of my gimlet-eyed mother, I flourished in my Yiddish environment in the company of my four cousins. I also learned to play the only game at which I was not a complete klotz: tennis. It was then an aristocratic sport, played only in white at exclusive clubs. Their exclusivity was confirmed by their total ban of Jews, that we accepted as a fact of life and yet another piece of bigotry practiced by hotels, housing subdivisions, banks, insurance companies, universities, and countless other gentile establishments owned and operated by worshippers of a Hebrew son of God.

In those pre-Holocaust days, we accepted discrimination as the price of living in Canada, knowing we had to work harder, longer, and smarter to succeed. The small Ottawa Jewish community, barred from sullying the clay courts of Christian tennis players, built their own establishment on the banks of the Rideau River, defiantly named the Tel Aviv Tennis Club. This pale imitation of their exclusively Christian premises was accessed by crossing a rickety wooden footbridge that never survived the icy winters. The limited, dilapidated Tel Aviv facilities were alive with camaraderie, kibitzing, fun, and delicatessen sandwiches that I have never seen equalled in alcohol-fueled gentile clubs that I visited as racial restrictions gradually eased.

The summer passed quickly and agreeably. My cousins, Esther, David, Lionel, and Eli were amiable company. Being engrossed in my budding architectural career I saw little of them thereafter, but our contact was nourished by their Ma's faithful liver transport. With time, the three Rabin boys were transformed into professionals and abandoned Ottawa for lusher pastures.

The eldest, David, studied metallurgy at McGill University in Montreal at the same time I pursued an architectural career on the same campus. Although the war was winding down, we were obliged to continue our military training at an army base for two weeks during the summer break. Many of us took this training less seriously than our officers demanded; among them was my cousin, David.

He and thirty others decided to study for their degree instead of writing a military exam; he was expelled. David had accepted a summer job in a copper mine in the Yukon, but he remained in Ottawa to plead for re-instatement. Fortunately, he found local employment as a rodman with a land surveyor. To his great relief, David was re-admitted in time for McGill's fall session, but not before he had realized that measuring building lots in fresh air was vastly preferable to stumbling around in dark, wet mining shafts that snaked through the bowels of the earth. He received his metallurgy degree, but worked every summer with a transit, level, and measuring tape, returning to school for an additional year to qualify as a surveyor. Metals and mines were forgotten; David established a profitable surveying office in Montreal. He blesses that military exam; it was the best test he never passed.

His first wife, Eleanor Namerow, died young from cancer that attacked even those with the temerity to marry into our family. Their son, Lawrence, carries on the surveying practice, and their daughter, Marilyn, is a dietician, a profession unknown to our clan. To the consternation of our family, David re-married. The second wife was a Québécoise, but time passed and relations normalized. He successfully defeated colon cancer, survived a stroke, retired, and plays golf.

His brothers entered their professions less dramatically. Lionel inherited his father's interest in liver and is a practicing pathologist in Washington, specializing in that organ. Eli, the youngest brother, also a doctor, is a leading kidney specialist in St. Catharines.

Their older sister, Esther, married Lawrence Bilsky, whose heart didn't meet military standards. It gave out when he was young and his widow raised their two daughters before she too died of our family curse. *Freg nisht.*

After Yosef's death Sochie was confined to her home with a back ailment.

While so immobilized and unable to leave her bed, she awoke in the middle of the night to perceive the dim image of a burglar ransacking her room. With a mighty shriek, she levitated from her mattress, seized her purse and bolted through the front door onto the street, throwing the purse under the closest parked vehicle. The

terrified burglar dived through the rear window which he had
entered and very likely abandoned his life of crime.

Sochie's cure was not permanent. She was ultimately brought to
Montreal's Neurological Hospital, a bastion of non-Jewish nerve specialists, where she was examined by a succession of doctors, residents, and their students. At the end of just such a group visit, as the
room began to empty, Sochie perceived that her full set of false teeth
that she had carefully stored on the night table had vanished.

"Meina tzainer," she lisped in pure Lithuanian Yiddish, "Voo
zenan meina tzainer!" ("Where are my teeth?")

As the dimensions of the loss became apparent, the learned
neurologists, with their residents and students, crawled over the
floor, picked through the bedclothes and fumbled through the mattress. They found nothing. As they turned to go, the mystery resolved
itself. One of the doctors had perched on the table and the teeth had
fastened themselves to his underside. Sochie could eat again.

Sochie survived the usual family cancer and lived many years
before her heart gave out. She was always a joy to be with: I'll never
forget her visit to my first home, barely completed and located on a
dirt road that led to a mud-filled pathway two feet below the entrance
door sill. As I lifted her in, I heard her mutter in her colloquial
Yiddish: "If this is heaven, take me to hell." That was Sochie: always
with the mot juste that made me smile.

In 1984 Sochie was called to join her Yosef and thirteen years
later was followed by her daughter. The sons continue with their
estimable careers, paying close attention to the injunction: be fruit-
ful and multiply. They have been enriched with wonderful children
and grandchildren; their forebears would be proud. I love and treasure them and pass on these notes that others may also do so.

Nathan: The Professor

Nathan, born in 1900, was two years younger than Pa. Unlike his
older brothers, he was never attracted to commerce; he was an academic, living in the lofty world of ideas. He saw the world as a complex organism, responding to primal needs, to economic necessity,
to political strife. I modelled my thinking after his; aside from Ma,

he influenced me more than anyone else. Nathan remained in Montreal for only a few of my early years before launching a successful pedagogic career in New York.

I include excerpts from his short memoir describing his early years in Galicia until he finished *gimnasium* that would prepare him for university. He also dictated a number of tapes describing this period; ten of these fascinating records survive, and I have preserved them on CDs for future generations.

I often listen to his voice. He is beside me; his dry, pedagogic tones are leavened with love, family lore, and humour. They tell of his childhood and his irresistible attraction to learning in the context of family, religious background, social climate, and political cataclysm. Unfortunately they do not deal with his later illustrious career. His written and spoken words are the only recorded eyewitness account that remains of our family's life in that time and place before it was cruelly destroyed.

The Reich family was from Terszow, not then, or ever, a major European centre. It was a dismal village that gave poverty new meaning. The Jewish inhabitants, mostly related by birth or marriage, clung to their religion, praying for the Messiah to deliver them; there was no other hope. Universities, professions, and emigration were almost inaccessible to them.

> There were not enough Jews in the village to have either a *cheder* or a house of worship and we depended on the adjoining village of Spas, that, reinforced by worshipers from other adjoining villages, had enough Jews to support a small synagogue with regular Shabbat and holiday services. Because the distance between these settlements exceeded what was permissible to walk on the Sabbath, it was necessary to construct a ritually acceptable "house" so that Jews could walk there, and thence continue to the synagogue without transgressing recognized tradition. The "house" consisted of several posts and beams, furnished with a few plates. The Almighty was placated and everyone's conscience was clear. Of course, the community could afford no rabbi, no cantor, no *bal koire*—all these functions were performed by volunteers of varying degrees of ability and inability. Indeed, the rivalries, jealousies, and personal animosity that attended the ultimate assignments of these functions were the subject of constant gossip, that sometimes rivalled the zeal of the services.

Nathan (The Professor) Reich left the only eyewitness account of our family's life in Europe before it was destroyed.

The Reich family was one of the few that owned and cultivated a small farm. Supplementary income was from modest enterprises, including sale of tobacco, liquor, and lumber; other relatives operated a grocery store and whatever else that capable of producing a few *groschen*. The *mishpocha* consisted of:

Zaida Avrum Moishe Hartman, his energetic and busy wife, Bobe Blume, a widowed grandmother, Rirtche, who, blind in her older years, spent her time reciting by heart every page of Tihilim and knitting socks for the entire family. My father, Shulem, was a city feller who married into the farm and shunned farm work and left it all to the womenfolk and occasional hired hands. He was a learned man: sociable, witty, interested in community activities. My mother, Leah, a quiet, pious, gentle woman born and raised on the farm, carried all the responsibilities of farm work and the household.

We were six siblings. The oldest brother, Yitzhak attended cheder and yeshiva until he married. The two sisters, Chaya and Chava, helped in running the household and in taking care of the three younger brothers, Mordkhe, Hirsch, and myself, Nute.

In the shtetels of Galicia, religion was central to family life, and rabbinical loyalties were strong. My father was raised by his father as an ardent Belzer Chassid, but in time turned away from its rigid, ascetic philosophy and lifestyle and felt at home in a more relaxed version. We youngsters hung around, joining in the singing and dancing that were a part of the services. The dancing was so fervent and intense that there was a saying among the peasants "Where Chassidim dance, grass will never grow."

Two of my cousins, Herman Reich, son of Pa's brother, Yitzhak, and Henry Nartzisenfeld (Field) son of Pa's sister, Chaya, immigrated to Canada before 1939. Only Blima Stein, daughter of another sister, Chava, survived; all the others, with their extended families, were murdered. I never met any of them or heard their voices; they exist only on a few faded photographs. Their brutal deaths had a profound effect on Nathan. (See picture on page 181.)

The *Cheder* Student

When Nathan was three, it was time for him to join his brothers who were attending *cheder*.

Terszow was too small to support a school and the closest facility was in Altshtut, a town of about two thousand, about one-third of whom were Jewish. It had some historical interest and was distinguished by several synagogues and *cheders*, the best of which was run by Moshe Mendel Itziks. However, it was about two kilometers distant and would involve walking to and from *cheder* every day in all weathers and seasons, often in the dark. Regular transportation did not exist and night accommodation was unavailable. A solution was found: the *Rebbe*, and more importantly his *Rebbitzin*, were persuaded to cook and care for the children during the week. His *cheder* life, typically followed on the benches of many generations of young Jewish scholars, is recorded here.

> I joined my brothers in the weekly pilgrimage to the *cheder*. To me this venturing out into the wider world was a source both of elation and apprehension. When my older brothers had left for the week, I felt lonely. I was the only child—everybody was engaged in household chores. Although we were natives of the village for several generations, there was practically no social contact with the gentile neighbors. So I literally counted the days until Friday when the return of my brothers made me jump all over the place. But on the other hand when my time came for leaving home for the *cheder*, I was seized by a terrific longing

for my mother. I was the youngest, and there was strong mutual attach-ment between mother and me.

However, the sense of duty prevailed and I joined my two brothers with bags of food on the walk to the *cheder*. The *cheder* was typical of that period. The curriculum, that had been established centuries ago, consisted of the study of prayers, *chumesh*, and *gemura*. The study was by rote. There were no examinations except for the custom of parents testing their children informally on Shabbat.

Rebbe Moishe Mendel Itziks was a kind, even-tempered man and in Altshtut his method of teaching was considered modern. From time to time, he gave us free time to learn and practice the art of letter writ-ing to parents and relatives. He regularly clipped our fingernails and carefully collected the nails and burned them or buried them in the cemetery. He even, at times, weather permitting, took us off the stud-ies and led us outdoors into the adjoining woods. We enjoyed this rest very much, though we occasionally ran into trouble with gangs of neighborhood *shkotzim*. Since he was not known for physical bravery and we were not itching for physical encounters with the more robust gentile kids, we always managed a discreet strategic retreat.

The *rebbe* seldom hit the children, although in case of serious breaches of discipline he was not totally disarmed. His tool was a sleeve. Because the room temperature on cold winter days was on the chilly side, he was dressed in a cotton-padded jacket. That jacket had seen many years of wear. In the course of the years, the cotton pads moved down to the end of the sleeve and, inasmuch as the sleeve also served the purpose of napkin and was used to wipe his mouth after eating, to wipe the sweat from his face, or wipe water accidentally spilt on the table, the pads hardened into a knot that, when it landed on a kid's shoulders, sent a serious message to the culprit.

But the *rebbe* rarely used any kind of physical punishment. He con-trolled the children by words, persistent piercing looks, and patience. The real power behind the throne was the *rebbetzin*. Her name was Hene, but her face was rewarded or punished by a pert button nose and she was generally referred to by young and old as Hene Nasel. She was the opposite of her husband. She was fast, sharp and domineer-ing, and stood for no nonsense from the occasionally rowdy and bois-terous kids. Her mere presence in the nearby kitchen, whose door she always kept open, was effective in maintaining order in the room.

The Public School Student

Cheder was succeeded by public school. The milieu was different; students were exposed to gentile teachers, a Catholic ambiance, and political tremors.

> I followed my two brothers and the other children of school age and entered the first year of the public school. This was a new experience, The atmosphere was strange. Although the Jewish children formed a substantial minority, they felt isolated from the rest of the children. Austria-Hungary was a Catholic country and, although the school was supported by taxes from citizens of all faiths, the Catholic religion was the dominant influence. In entering my classroom on the first day I was shocked to see a crucifix on the wall. Every morning the school session started with the Pater Nostra in Polish. Although Jewish children were exempt from reciting the prayer, we were required to stand at attention. The rebbe advised us not to listen, but, while God in his wisdom allowed for closing the eyes to avoid irritating sights, he did not provide for a convenient closing of the ears, and after listening two hundred times to the prayer during the first school year, all Jewish kids knew it by heart—a prayer that I still remember after the passing of seventy years.

The *Gimnasium* Student

Six years of public school usually marked the end of formal schooling of Jewish children of Nathan's time and place. Advanced education was selected by relatively few families, usually wealthier or more assimilated. Admission to university required more years in a *gimnasium*, and was subject to passing a demanding entrance examination. Parents predisposed to orthodoxy did not promote this option.

> The nearest *gimnasium* was in Sambor, a larger city about twenty kilometers from Terszow. Orthodox Jews overwhelmingly opposed sending their children to *gimnasium*. They feared estrangement from traditional Jewish life. Shabbat attendance was obligatory. The studies claimed more time and to that extent encroached upon the time available for the cultivation of the study of the Bible and Talmud. With due modesty, I was the first boy from an Orthodox family to be set on going to *gimnasium*.

Sure enough, when I first raised the question Zaida Avorum Moishe responded with a loud "no." Father, who married into the family, while not strongly opposed, found it the better part of wisdom to stay neutral. Mother, who always liked to be on my good side, did not dare to oppose her father, but secretly was pleased with Zaida's opposition. She dreaded my prolonged absences from home and feared for my health, as I was physically underdeveloped. In view of the opposition, I could not muster the strength to force the issue. I gave up the idea for the time being, entered the fifth year of the elementary school and bided my time.

I had hoped that persistence would eventually sway Zaida to say "yes." It did not sway him. Providence interfered, and grandfather died in 1911. I was shocked and saddened. I dearly loved him and he was one of the kindest men in my little world. But after a period of genuine mourning, I reopened my request. Father, after a show reluctance to satisfy his allegiance to the Orthodox fraternity, agreed.

I quit the fifth year, reduced my *cheder* hours and started preparing for the test of admittance late summer. I had little concern about most of the subject matter that formed the substance of the test, but my concern was the Polish language, particularly its pronunciation. I had little occasion to speak Polish. We learned it in school, I occasionally heard it on the streets, but never heard it spoken at home and, in the intensely nationalist climate, the admission authorities assigned high importance to correct Polish pronunciation in deciding admission to the school.

My father, who I suspected all along favored my plan, took a certain pride in my determination and provided me with a Polish tutor, a son of one of the Polish officials with whom he had some business contacts, who was a dropout from the university, but spoke perfect Polish.

For several months, I spent two hours daily just conversing. He was quite a playboy, was flattered that he was given this assignment, admired my determination to defy Orthodox Jewish opinion and assured me that he would spend all his free time from February to August to see me through. And see me through he did.

By August, I was ready to face the music. There was one little obstacle—my *payes*. While there was no law that *payes* could not be worn in *gimnasium*, I was apprehensive that with my rustic, small-town appearance, my still imperfect Polish pronunciation would not be enhanced by my showing up with pendant *payes*. I was afraid to cut them off before the test, for, should I fail, I would have to return to Altshtut and face the dirty looks of my peers and utter contempt of my elders. Here my two sisters Chaya and Chava, who were very much in my corner, rose to the occasion. They shortened and thinned the *payes* a little and with the aid of thick prune juice combed them behind the ears. In the excitement of the test atmosphere, the sidetracked *payes* escaped the attention of the examiners. I passed, and was the first boy from Moishe Mendel Itziks' *cheder* and from the Orthodox community who was admitted to the *gimnasium*.

After the test, I promptly cut the *payes*. The finale of the *payes* story came two weeks later on Rosh Hashanah when I came home to celebrate the New Year with my family. I donned the civilian clothes that I wore in *cheder* but I obviously could not restore the *payes*. As we were walking, we met one of the elders of the Beltzer group. He was the self-appointed guardian of the religious and moral conduct of the children and grandchildren of his crony, Hersch Reich, my paternal grandfather. My father's desertion from the Beltzer family and now my father's acquiescence in my dereliction "avek tzi di goyim" was too much for the old man. He passed along, stopped for a moment, cast a contemptuous glance at my father and spat at me. Under those auspicious circumstances, I entered my academic career.

The course of education in those times and places was bedevilled by competing nationalist ambitions that finally precipitated the collapse of the Austria-Hungarian Empire. I recorded earlier that Galicia was inhabited by Poles who ruled in most cities and by Ukrainians who enjoyed overwhelming majorities in rural areas. In between was a significant minority of Jews, who were beloved by neither. As fortunes of war fluctuated, Jews made excellent scapegoats and were enthusiastically looted, raped, or killed by either side. This was not new to history and set the stage for worse to come.

There was a law in Galicia that the language spoken at home was a factor in the choice of language of instruction of a particular school. The Polish minority, more educated, and more heavily represented in the professions, particularly in the civil service, fought bitterly and on the whole successfully for courses to be taught in Polish in as many schools as possible. The Ukrainians, in their newly aroused nationalism, charged that since they constituted the majority of the school districts the Ukrainian language should be the chosen language. And to ascertain the actual situation the educational authorities instituted from time to time language censuses. This created a dilemma for the Jewish students. Those from thoroughly assimilated homes readily gave

Polish as their mother tongue The majority of Jewish students, however, who were eager to assert their national feeling, gave Yiddish as their mother tongue. The Austrian government did not grant to Yiddish the status of an independent language. We then agreed to declare Hebrew as our mother tongue, but principals knew quite well that we did not speak Hebrew at home and rejected our declarations as not accurate. The stalemate was simply resolved by the principal who, in the privacy of his office, counted all the Jewish students as coming from homes where Polish was spoken, and falsely created a Polish majority that provided the legal justification for retaining the Polish language of instruction, in gross violation of the rights of the Ukrainians who clearly formed the majority in the district.

The Austria-Hungarian Empire collapsed. We were plunged into a state of political chaos. Hundreds of thousands of Russian war prisoners walked out of their camps and, wending their way home, looted and plundered. The governments—federal, provincial and municipal—ceased to exist.

The Poles and the Ukrainians, completely settled in their territories, promptly claimed their historic rights. The Poles proclaimed their independence and the more than three million Ukrainians announced the establishment of the Western Ukrainian Republic. The Polish population offered a military challenge to the fledgling Ukrainian Republic and routed the Ukrainian forces. The Jews tried to maintain neutrality and were hit by both sides and several hundred Jews lost their lives, mainly the victims of Polish soldiery. The Ukrainians retreated and managed to establish a semblance of orderly government in the rest of Eastern Galicia. Schools were re-opened and there was some restoration of normal economic life.

The attendance was sharply reduced by the complete boycott of the Polish students who went into hiding and fled westward to join the Polish army that was mobilizing for a general attack on the fledgling Ukrainian Republic. Absent, too, were the Polish teachers. The language of instruction became Ukrainian and their Jewish students, as well as the teachers, went through a painful process of adjustment.

But the relative peace did not last. In 1919, the Poles, several times more numerous and militarily better equipped, routed the Ukrainians. Polish power was promptly restored over the province. The Ukrainian students and teachers fled. The Poles came out of hiding and rejoiced The Jews accepted the inevitable and hoped for the best.

Among the first to suffer were the Jewish students who had attended the school and the Jewish teachers who continued to teach during the Ukrainian regime. The Polish Government interpreted these acts as approaching treason to the new Polish Republic that had never renounced historical claim to these territories. Jewish students who applied to the now re-opened Polish schools were summarily expelled one month before the final examination—the *matura*—that entitled one to enter the university. The few Jewish teachers were suspended.

We Jewish students were stunned by the action of the Polish authorities. For a time we thought that almost eight years of study and hope had been wiped out by the stroke of a hostile pen. But the situation was not as hopeless as it first appeared. Local lawyers dispensed an Austria-Hungarian law that gave every person the right to present himself for the *matura*, even though he had not attended school for a day, provided, of course, he mastered the required knowledge. We learned that sons of Orthodox Jewish parents who did not like the *goyish* atmosphere of the *gimnasium* worked on their own or with the help of tutors, and that, for other reasons, some very wealthy people preferred to employ private tutors to prepare their children for the final examination. The law was applicable in the territories of the dismembered Austria-Hungarian Empire. We availed ourselves of the law, applied to the proper authorities, and obtained the status of externs, as such candidates were called.

The twenty or so students got busy and organized study groups, We had some help from the Jewish professors who, now suspended from teaching, were only too glad to help. While we were preparing, news filtered through that most of the examiners would be our own Polish teachers—news that brought us great relief and stimulated us to greater effort to do well. And we did well! Apparently the professors did not take the cause for our expulsion very seriously. We all passed, some even with distinction.

The University Student

Nathan was now qualified to enter a university. But where? Marcus and Harry had established themselves in Montreal and were struggling to start a business. Canada, a land of opportunity, attracted Nathan. Pa made the necessary arrangements: Nathan was sponsored by a newly invented cousin, Aaron Nirenberg, who deposed:

> I am in a good financial standing having an amount of $15,000 in the bank and well furnished house and great deal of assets..... I will take

care of him while in Canada and that he shall not become a burden to Canada or any province or village.

Canada, persuaded by the fifteen-thousand-dollar guarantee, agreed. Despite his mother's pleadings, Nathan travelled to Canada on a student's visa. He arrived in Halifax in January 1923, and, being certified free of trachoma and lice by the doctor of The Cunard Steam Ship Company, was permitted to land. His excellent record of achievement at the *gimnasium* in Sambor for eight years gained him admittance to McGill University. That he spoke no English was not a deterrent; newly arrived immigrants from Eastern Europe, spurred by necessity, were quick learners. To finance his stay he became a teacher at the Jewish People's School. Unfortunately many of its students were poor and the struggling institution lacked money. Nathan seldom received his pay, but his employment produced an unexpected bonus. He met and eventually married Riva Rudy, a fellow teacher.

Despite his feeble grasp of newly acquired English, Nathan entered university that autumn. He studied economics under Professor Stephen Leacock whose academic work has long been forgotten, but who lives on as one of Canada's greatest humourists. Leacock took a liking to the spunky immigrant and helped him, as described in an undated *Reader's Digest* article by Senator Eugene Forsey.

The German Student

Leacock had a phenomenal capacity for languages quite apart from anything else. A Polish Jew came into our class in the third year who had seven languages but neither English or French. Leacock dealt with this by saying now and again in a lecture "Verstehen sie, Herr Reich?" "Nein, Herr Professor"[1] Then Leacock would give him a short summary in excellent German of what he had just been saying. "Verstehen sie jetzt, Herr Reich?" "Jawohl, Herr Professor."[2]

Nathan's one weakness was English literature, of which he knew nothing. He approached his teacher and explained his problem. The professor, favourably inclined to the new student, promised to

1. Now do you understand, Mr. Reich? No, Mr. Professor
2. Do you understand now? Yes, Mr. Professor,

Odcinek ten pozostaje u pasażera.

THE CUNARD STEAM SHIP COMPANY LIMITED

Marszałkowska 154, W A R S A W.

№ 2023)

The undermentioned passenger has this day been examined by the **Cunard Line** Doctor
Name *Reich   Natan*
Age *22* Ticket Number *57374*
Passenger was found to be free from
TRACHOMA — FAVUS .
and was generally in a healthy condition.
Passenger has been vaccinated and is free from lice.
Signature of Doctor
Date 1 4. XII. 1922

Nathan was certified free of lice, vaccinated, and free
of Trachoma-Favus when he landed in Halifax.

do what he could, but Nathan had to write the examination. Nathan obliged. The only question he recognized concerned the English poem format known as the sonnet. He devoted his test answer to a full explanation of the form and beauty of the Polish sonnet. He passed.

Nathan mastered the language quickly, thanks to innate talent and a solid foundation of Latin and Greek. He received his Bachelor of Arts degree in 1925, his Master's degree a year later, and looked forward to post-graduate school with the possibility of joining McGill's faculty. His chosen field was economics. He received the following letters on McGill University stationery.

Dear Mr. Reich,

Yes of course I remember you well as one of our best students. But I can't advise you to come. Owing to your national origin you'd have very little chance to get anything proportional to your academic merit. This is not my fault. And before you get angry about it, ask yourself what kind of a good ghost of a chance I would have in the Ukraine district of Soviet Russia. But if I can help you in any other way let me know.

Stephen Leacock

November 25, 1929

Dear Mr. Reich,

I remember you very well indeed and it did not need a letter from you to make me recall your name. I remember how quickly you picked up English and also the very excellent standing you made in our department.

Now to come to your query. I am sorry to say that I think your chance of obtaining a position in Canada is not very good. I am the more sorry because Canada is my country and I regret very much the prejudice against Jews that exists here. I think that your chances are infinitely better in the United States especially in academic work.

Yours very truly,

J.C . Arminion

The Savant

The situation was clear. Despite being recognized as "one of the best students" who "picked up English quickly" and being praised for his "very excellent standing in the department," Nathan's Canadian career was over before it had started. McGill University would be closed to him.

He briefly considered law as an option and attended l'Université de Montréal for a year. By then his visa had expired and deportation threatened. He had been reminded that the United States was more favourably disposed to Jews and accepted a post as Research Fellow at the University of Chicago. The brothers Reich posted a bond to ensure that he would not become a public charge. He never did.

McGill University

MONTREAL

Faculty of Arts
Department of Economics and
Political Science

Dear Mr Reich

Yes of course I remember you well as one of our best students. But I fear I can't advise you to come: owing to your national origin you'd have very little chance to get anything proportional to your academic merit. This is not my fault. — And before you get angry about it, ask yourself what kind of a good ghost of a chance would I have in the Ukrainian District of Soviet Russia. & .... But I I can

Luck you in any other way

believe me.

P.L.

Stephen Leacock

This letter signed by Stephen Leacock and another letter from McGill made it clear that, being a Jew, Nathan could not hope for a future at McGill or at other academic institutions in Canada.

Nathan subsequently taught at Brookings Institution and Howard University in Washington, then relocated to New York and for four years was Assistant Editor to the Encyclopedia of Social Sciences. And why not? Ten years earlier he spoke not a word of English.

In 1930 he registered at Columbia University. He received his Ph.D. in 1938 and was awarded the Seligman Prize and a Guggenheim Fellowship. By 1942 he was Acting Chairman, Department of Economics at Hunter College. He mediated labour problems, wrote books and articles, and lectured until his retirement in 1974.

Riva, a brilliant educator, directed principals of schools. She was warm, witty, worldly wise, and happy, seemingly unaffected by the cares that wore down other administrators. She was interesting and fun to be with. Despite these positive attributes, my mother never fully approved of her. Riva smoked; a cigarette drooped constantly from her lips and ashes spilled into whatever recipe she was following. When she visited us, Aunt Miriam followed her with a dustpan, collecting debris from her nicotine habit. Riva was not enthralled by housekeeping and was said to be a nonchalant cook. She had no children of her own, but adopted two: Danny and Judy. She was a perfect mate for Nathan and he never recovered from her death in 1978.

When possible, Nathan visited Montreal; we were his only family and he was close to his brothers. And I was close to him. I looked forward to his brief stays as a parched animal seeks a waterhole. I followed his every step, ceaselessly questioning him: politics, business, economics, history; everything, except sports, that he disdained. He was lucid, his arguments were irrefutable, and were buttressed by pertinent examples. I was captivated by his approach to world problems and to his analytical powers. I wanted to be like him, but not only mentally; I never trimmed my eyebrows so that they would better match his bushy professorial brows, hoping that some of his wisdom would rub off on me.

In Montreal he visited old friends and lectured at Jewish institutions. A true professor, he needed no time to prepare a speech on any topic; he only required an audience. I recall a talk he was scheduled to give at the local Young Men's Hebrew Association before a large assembly to be attended by community leaders and other notables. It would receive press attention. He made no notes for his lecture, but spent the afternoon at our house, relaxing with the family and enjoying ever-present tea and cakes. Marcus, a bundle of nerves at the best of times and a renowned worrier, refused to attend the talk; he feared Nathan would stumble out, apologize for his lack of words and expire from humiliation. He needn't have worried. Nathan, if awakened from a sound sleep, could readily deliver an impromptu discourse on economics, politics, and international affairs. He taught me the importance of a ready tongue, and I took the lesson to heart.

My contacts with Nathan were limited to such short visits. But on one grand occasion I travelled to see him. The war had cut off any possibility of seeing the outside world. Television didn't exist, films were heavily censored, and, in Quebec, movie houses could not admit anyone younger than sixteen. Libraries had lists of banned books. I desperately longed to travel, to explore. It wasn't until I was sixteen that I made my first visit to New York. As an unworldly, unsophisticated hayseed, I thrilled to that city's magnificent skyline, to Manhattan's streets pulsing with people, flashing with lights, and lined with incredible stores. I marvelled at highways twisting around each other through the sky, and at ear-piercing subway trains that clattered between dingy stations lined with graffiti-decorated tiles.

Best of all, I stayed at Nathan's house in the Bronx. He took me everywhere: to museums, restaurants, and to my first extravaganza, a new Broadway production, *Oklahoma!* The theatre was my gateway to magic; the lights dimmed, the buzzing audience hushed, the curtain rose, a cowboy swaggered to the footlights, and, under a glorious stage sun glowing over a field of painted corn, he sang: *Oh what a beautiful morning!* My heart echoed. *Oh what a beautiful evening!* It was splendid—one of my happiest memories. I enjoyed many wonderful productions since, but there's only one first time.

My later trips to New York were never complete without visiting Nathan before and after his retirement from Hunter College. I never outgrew the pleasure of sitting at his feet, indulging my childhood compulsion to question, debate, and learn.

His insights were always useful. At the height of the Cold War with the USSR I recall discussing the Communist threat to civilization, where one country after another seemed on the brink of toppling into the socialist abyss. Their monolithic power and popular appeal appeared invincible. Fanned by alarms of Senator McCarthy and by crises in Cuba, Vietnam, Cambodia, Taiwan, and other unstable regions, international revolution seemed inevitable.

Nathan was sanguine. He was an expert on the economy of the USSR, had access to Soviet newspapers, and had spoken to many who had visited or lived there. He assured me that their entire structure was an unworkable sham, maintained only by terror. They could neither feed nor clothe their people, their products were shoddy and their Five Year Plans were fiction. Our best strategy would be to flood these benighted countries with Sears Catalogues. I was not convinced, but, after visiting the USSR, Hungary, and Bulgaria, I doubted him less. When the entire Communist structure collapsed into a heap of dust, he was vindicated. There was nothing left—less than nothing: morality, legality, trust, had all had been throttled by that terrible oppression. In the free world billions of dollars had been spent, thousands of lives sacrificed, and international diplomacy skewed by supporting dictators, all to control a non-existent threat. Everything had been wasted. Nathan had been right.

Pre-occupied by my own family and career, I saw less of him. Time passed. He retired from his platform at Hunter College. After Riva's death he lived a lonely life in his east Manhattan apartment. His children moved to other states. Their homes were open to him, but he stubbornly refused to leave his book-lined rooms and his diminishing circle of friends. His memory began to fail. Companions were required. In 1991 he succumbed suddenly to an aneurysm and now rests alongside his wife and brothers in a Montreal cemetery. He died, but not my memories of him. He was my hero. He still is.

Gathering information for this Memoir, I explored the website of YIVO, an organization with a vast database of origins of Jewish families. Searching the file of the town of Sambor, home of Nathan's *gimnasium*, I pressed my computer key: Nathan, in his school uniform, leaped out at me—it was 1918—he was young, but unmistakable. A chill ran down my spine. He was in my home. But the truth is he had never left me.

OUT OF THE ASHES

I had intended this Memoir to be a happy recollection of the lives of my family members and myself, but I cannot ignore the horrific but inspiring stories of those close to us who survived the Holocaust. I warn readers that this Chapter is painful and disturbing.

Destruction of a Family

Pa was twenty-two when he said farewell to his family in Europe. In those days emigrants and those left behind knew they would seldom, if ever, see each other again. There would be no long distance phone calls, no faxes, no email. Letters took months to arrive. Visits involved long trips in tossing ships and smoky trains and were expensive. Pa returned to the family home once in the 1930s. His father questioned him about America: he'd heard about the marvels of the "new world," even experienced electricity, telephones, and automobiles.

"How are taxes collected?" he wanted to know.

Pa explained. "Every year people fill out forms stating their income, calculate a percentage and send it to the government."

His father laughed in disbelief. "You tell the government what you earned and send them a percentage that you, yourself, calculate? Impossible!"

In that wretched corner of the earth a tax collector travelled from village to village. Anticipating his arrival, families drove their herds and flocks into the woods, buried their silver, and pleaded abject poverty because of weather, fire, plague, and other disasters, real or imaginary. The tax collector, no novice at these games, assessed what he could extract, took his bribe and departed until the next year. Life in that region was one of venality and insecurity.

Pa's family lived in an increasingly poisonous milieu. Local Ukrainian peasants and Polish town dwellers were bitter enemies, united only in hatred of their Jewish neighbours with whom they'd lived side by side for centuries.

Harry, Marcus, and Nathan, with youthful initiative and courage, had saved themselves from lives of poverty, insecurity, and, finally, extermination. But they couldn't save themselves from the guilt that accompanied their foresight. Depression shadowed their lives; worries normal to living and working were always exaggerated. Pa confided to me that nightmares disturbing his sleep always centred on deportation. Anxiety was never far below the surface.

The youngest sons had migrated; their parents, Shulem and Leah, with their older brother, Yitzhak and two sisters, Chaya and Chava, with their families, chose to remain at home until it was too late to extract them all from the inferno; only two nephews, Herman and Henry, arrived in Canada in the 1930s and were duly absorbed by The Store.

As war threatened, the rest of the family decided to follow. They sent pathetic letters telling of futile efforts to obtain papers permitting them to migrate, but bureaucracy and the implacable anti-Semitism of the Canadian government doomed them.

February 15, 1938

My dear Herman, live long!

.....The Goyim rejoice in the coming war. They wait for war like Jews wait for the Messiah. They have already begun to celebrate.....

March 5, 1938

Dear Herman,

.....you wrote about our coming to Canada.....we have decided to do it, barring any obstacles.....I still don't know if this is possible. I'm still not sure if we can do this, and how things will work out. The reason we decided to emigrate is the feeling of imminent war.....it will come sooner or later. Jews will feel the effects. The government is enforcing

Polanizing businesses, taking everything out of Jewish hands.....they don't allow me to earn a living.....

March 19, 1938

Dear Herman,

We are afraid there will be a war any minute, The Ukrainians are waiting. It is hard to imagine what will happen to the Jews.....

September 1938

Dear Herman,

.....war is hanging on a hair. There is no hope.....but maybe things will be resolved.....but we live in fear......no patience for anything else...... it is all very sad..... God help us.....

November 6, 1938

Dear Herman,

.....business is stagnant, prices are falling.....the Jewish situation is sad and catastrophic. All businesses are being taken out of Jewish hands and are being nationalized.....they say that we have been "guests" here for a long time.....

November 1938

Dear Nathan,

.....we cannot find a buyer for the house.....there is now a border and only Poles can buy and sell there. If a Jew buys, it is not a valid sale.....I'm convincing myself that I'm already with one foot out. Is this just fantasy? Once the idea of leaving seemed crazy, now it is the only thing I want.....who knows if it will ever happen You all know that we must leave.....

May 21, 1939

Dear brother,

.....you write to us about rumours of an alliance between Germany and Russia. Is it possible these rumours will become reality?.....God willing it will all end up for the best.....

August 1939

Dear Herman, live long!

.....there is nothing left to do.....it has been one year and a half since I began to talk about leaving this place. Now I see I have not made good. Who knows if it will ever happen.....who knows what tomorrow will bring.....the war is now inevitable. How the war will play out, who can imagine? Everyone is looking. Everyone is pessimistic. Every one looks at me like I'm crazy because I'm still here. Why am I not leaving?..... whatever will happen to everyone will happen to us too, You did what you could.....

Then there was silence; the silence of the grave.

★ ★ ★

The German invasion of Poland broke off contact with our family in Galicia. When hostilities ceased, Nathan took temporary leave from Hunter College to join the American Joint Distribution Committee, an organization bringing relief to Jewish survivors, re-uniting families, and re-locating refugees. He viewed at close range the devastation of the Holocaust and gleaned what details were available of the fate of his father, mother, brother, sisters, and their extended families. They'd been taken from their homes and murdered by the *Einsatzgruppen*, mobile killing units of the German SS. Often their Ukrainian neighbours were enthusiastic collaborators in the massacres and many welcomed the German invaders until they, in turn, became their victims. Nathan was haunted by what he had learned, and the rest of his life was plagued by bouts of depression.

Only Blima Stein, Pa's niece, had successfully hidden herself. Her sister, Regina, chose to pass as a gentile forced labourer and was never heard from again. The family was extinct. When the war ended, Blima came out of hiding and remembered her American Uncle Nathan. She addressed a letter to Dr. Reich, New York, that miraculously found its destination. We brought her to Montreal; she lived in our home until she married Sam Zimmet, also a Holocaust survivor.

Blima was blonde and blue-eyed, solidly built and energetic, full of life that she'd been denied during the period she'd passed as a

The Reich family in Terszow, circa 1935. All but four in this photo were killed in the following years. Top, l. to r., Chava Eva (Reich) Stein, Pa's sister; her husband David Stein; Herman Reich, Yitschak's son; Blima Narzisenfeld (Chaya's daughter) and Henry Narzisenfeld (Chaya's son); Pa's brothers Moshe and Yitschak Reich; and Chaya's husband, Melech Narzisenfeld. Middle, Pa's sister Chaya (Reich) Narzizenfeld; Pa's parents Leah and Sholem Reich; Celia (Feiler) Reich, Yitschak's wife; Uncle Nathan's wife, Riva Reich, who was visiting from New York. Bottom, Chava's daughters Regina and Blima Stein; Yitschak's son and daughter, Nathan and Rivka Reich. Pa's nephews Herman and Henry reached Canada in the 1930s before the doors were closed. Young Blima Stein survived and came to Canada in 1950.

gentile on a Polish farm. She gloried in her new-found secure world, rich beyond belief. Ma gave her a fur coat; she wore it for months, even when she slept. She never spoke to us of the family she'd lost, or of her perillous years. Her husband died in 1959, aged only thirty, leaving a son David. Blima re-married Jacob Zeimer, another survivor; they settled in Melbourne, Australia, and raised three sons, all successful professionals. She recently passed away, leaving many questions unanswered.

★ ★ ★

Others survived those terrible years and many found themselves in Montreal after the war. These included Miriam Brahms, who married Herman Reich, Pa's nephew, and Lisl Epstein, who married Sidney Ivry, Ma's brother.

Miriam and Lisl came out of the ashes of Europe destitute, their families destroyed, their friends scattered or dead. Their work experience, hard labour under guns of their oppressors, was not readily marketable. They were transplanted to a new language and culture. Despite the horrors they witnessed and the vicissitudes they endured, Miriam and Lisl lived to create new families and rejoice in their children and grandchildren. They also contributed, each in her own way, to the communities that received them.

Each composed a memoir that describes her ordeals, the only written testimony from our family of that terrible period; I can find no better words than those of Miriam and Lisl to pass on their message.

Miriam Brahms Reich

Miriam Brahms was born in Lithuania in 1930. The small Baltic state had been part of Russia until the end of the First World War, and was home to about two hundred and fifty thousand Jews. The largest city, Kaunas, included about forty thousand Jews, comprising one quarter of its population.

Miriam's father, Reuven Abramovitch, was a wholesale importer of cloth. His successful business allowed his wife, children and parents, and Miriam's grandparents, with hired help, to live in two homes on a large property surrounded by a sizable garden. They spent summers in a *dacha*. Life was sweet.

In June 1940, Miriam was celebrating her tenth birthday. The party was outdoors, in the gazebo of their garden. Her mother, father, and a brother, older by two and a half years, were enjoying strawberries and cream when they heard a commotion in the street. It was the arrival of the Red Army invading Lithuania in accordance with a pact between two of history's greatest criminals, Joseph Stalin and Adolph Hitler. The army did not resist and the local population waved and cheered.

With the Soviet invasion, family life immediately changed. Their business was confiscated and the family was forced to share their home with others. Everything of value was seized; seven thousand Jews, deemed enemies of the state, were deported to the Soviet Union. Miriam's Hebrew *gimnasium* was closed and she was sent to a school where all subjects were taught in Russian.

There was worse to come; much worse.

A year later the Stalin-Hitler pact was shattered as German armies crossed the frontier and quickly occupied the country. New regulations dehumanizing, terrorizing, and humiliating Jews were enacted: they were to wear yellow badges; they were forbidden to walk on the pavement, use public transportation, or own a car, radio or property. They were not allowed to frequent public parks or playgrounds or visit theaters, movies, libraries or museums.

The slaughter began. Local nationalist-fascist groups that had mobilized during the Soviet occupation joined with Lithuanian police and German mobile killing units, known as *Einsatzgruppe*, to inaugurate the Final Solution. By the end of December one hundred and eighty thousand Lithuanian Jews had been massacred, including ten thousand in Kaunas. They were picked up in the streets or at their homes, made to dig their own graves, and executed. The Catholic Church in Lithuania forbade help to the Jews and members of the clergy sent Hitler a congratulatory note on the event of the invasion.

In her memoir, *I Pick Up My Life and Take It With Me*, Miriam describes the indescribable:

Since it was not safe for a Jew to be seen on the streets and we needed food to survive, I removed my yellow star and went out to shop for essentials. It was a challenge and a necessity; my family depended on me. I didn't look Jewish and was able to pass as a gentile. I was eleven.

On July 9, 1941, the Nazis ordered that a ghetto be completed within four weeks. On August 15 the remaining Jews of Kaunas found themselves inside the ghetto in the suburb of Slobodka, surrounded by barbed wire guarded by posts manned by Lithuanians. It contained almost thirty thousand Jews.

Labour brigades were organized. The lucky ones, including my father, were put to work. Food was scarce. We were paid in rations that were at a starvation level.

Worst of all were the periodic *aktionen*. At dawn, a loud alarm would sound; every man, woman, and child had to leave their houses and assemble on a large field. The SS, with their dogs, clubs and bayonets would be waiting for us. Then the selection process began, sending people to the left or the right. We tried to look healthy by pinching our cheeks to get some colour, to walk straight and appear confident in order to impress the SS, but at five in the morning and scared to death of the fate that awaited us, it was a task that few accomplished. I dreaded these *aktionen*, not only for myself but for my family. My paternal grandparents were elderly, not well and therefore at very high risk. Usually the old, the weak, and the sick would be motioned to one side, and occasionally some young ones. Those who didn't move quickly enough were beaten or shot. In the *aktionen* of October 28, 1941, nine thousand were executed, half of them children. Our luck held. My parents, brother and I were once again motioned to join the group that would remain in the ghetto—for the time being.

How did I deal with such terror? Since I was powerless to change the situation I assumed a fatalistic approach. Numbness set in. I put my feelings on hold and became an observer, distancing myself from time and place, a Chagallesque image hovering in space, at the same time remaining very vigilant and aware of the precariousness of the situation. Each moment presented a new danger, a new challenge. It was also easier to face the possibility of death when you saw people dying around you. It became the norm rather than the exception. There were public executions, shootings, torture, little food, and a constant stream of frightening rumours. I saw my first public hanging. I vividly remember a small puddle forming underneath the gallows; my father explained.

The future, if there was to be one, was unpredictable and bleak.

Conditions changed in the autumn of 1943. The ghetto became a concentration camp. On March 27, 1944, one thousand eight hundred persons, consisting primarily of children and elderly men and women were dragged out of their houses and murdered. By the beginning of April, fewer than eighteen thousand Jews were left in the ghetto. On October 26, 1943, a large part of the population was evacuated. It started with an early morning assembly. Once more the difference between life and death was determined by an almost imperceptible motion of a leather gloved hand or an impatient shout to hurry up accompanied by a shove, a blow on the head or a kick by a highly polished, black boot. Occasionally a shot would be heard that felled a laggard. Thousands of us lined up, slowly advancing to our judgment. Facing the stream of humanity were SS men and Lithuanian guards who made sure that nothing would interfere with their efficient participation in the Final Solution.

This time, their operations were conducted more methodically. Men were separated from women, old and frail were grouped together, children were separated from parents. Those who clung to them were forced to give them up and the children who hung on to their parents were one by one plucked off like vermin and carried screaming to the waiting trucks. Parents volunteering to accompany their children were beaten and shoved towards their assigned sections. How do you describe the cries of a child snatched away from a mother's embrace? The weeping and wailing and screaming were sounds and sights that will remain with me until I die.

I did not know what my fate would be. I was thirteen. I looked older than my years and when my turn came the SS must have considered me a productive adult. My mother and I became part of a large group to be sent to a concentration camp in Estonia. My father and brother were dispatched to another campWe never saw each other again.

We later learned that on August 4, 1944, my frail father, at another selection, was directed to the side of the doomed. My brother, unwilling to leave him, pretended to suffer from a bad knee and begged to join him. His wish was granted. The group was taken to a nearby forest and shot. Their bodies were burned.

The train ride lasted a week. The sanitary conditions were indescribable: hardly any food, very little water, and no air. The grieving mothers who lost their children were inconsolable. It was hell.

We arrived at Camp Kurame in Estonia; the weather deteriorated as winter approached. Rain was heavy and mud was knee deep. After two years in the ghetto our clothing was in tatters and we limped on wood-soled shoes. Dysentery was common, along with a host of other diseases. We had no running water, no toilets—only an outhouse and a well. We slept on tiers of boards, bundled in our day clothes. The smell in the bunks, especially at night, was odious. We did what we could to keep clean, but most of the time it was too cold to undress and bathe. Looking for lice in the seams of our clothes was the common evening recreational activity.

No matter how sick we were, we would go to work. Staying in the barracks was a death sentence. We returned to camp a after a day's labour and people would be missing; they were never heard of again.

We lined up at dawn in the camp square to be counted, often several times. Thin gruel was ladled from a large kettle into a bowl to each prisoner. After "breakfast" we assembled into work crews and marched to build roads that led nowhere. We cleared trees, dug road beds, and spread gravel—all manually. The midday "meal" consisted of cabbage soup with a few potatoes. We returned to our bunks to more of the same, with a slice or two of bread. Work was a privilege, our only hope of staying alive.

We remained at that camp until mid-winter. The Russians were advancing and we were re-located to another Estonian camp. We walked for three days over non-existing roads, half starved, in the depth of winter, dressed in tatters, wearing wooden shoes. Those who fell, or were too exhausted to take another step, were shot. You couldn't stop to help the fallen unless you were prepared to give up your own life. What did you do? You donned imaginary blinders, faced front, put one foot before another and became totally absorbed in your own survival. At one point my mother lost her will and strength to continue. Upon my relentless urging, she carried on until we reached our destination, Camp Goldfiels.

Life became somewhat easier. The weather improved, the guards were a little friendlier, the days were longer, brighter and warmer. And we heard rumours of the advancing Russian army. My memories of that camp would be better except for a tragedy.

I met a girl my age. On a beautiful spring day we struck up a conversation with a young Estonian guard and asked permission to walk down the road. He granted our request. We had scarcely gone five hundred feet when a shot hit my friend in the stomach. I dragged her back to the camp. She bled profusely and I could see her intestines protrud-

Miriam (Brahms) Reich at Bergen-Belsen in 1946. She arrived in Montreal on December 11, 1947.

ing. She died in a couple of hours. No one asked what happened; it was as if it had never occurred. It remains a powerful memory that I kept to myself all these years.

In autumn 1944, the Russians were advancing and we were again put into box cars and taken to Germany. From the train I observed the peaceful, idyllic scenes of the German countryside. To this day I still taste the longing I felt for a life free of terror, squalor and hunger—it was a glimpse of what life could be like.

Mother and I found ourselves in a camp in Stutthof. Our heads were shaved and we were transferred yet again to Okenzoll, near Hamburg, where I filed metal parts for guns in a munitions factory under the supervision of a kindly Belgian prisoner. Conditions improved. I worked inside, it was warm, and I was entitled to a glass of milk every day.

Allied armies continued to advance. In February 1945, the SS transferred us to Bergen-Belsen. I'd survived seventeen months in the ghetto and twenty-eight months in concentration camps, experiencing the worst in human degradation and German depravity. I thought it couldn't be worse and that nothing could shock me. I was wrong.

Arriving in Bergen-Belsen I was de-loused, had my head shorn, and was clad in a striped uniform. Although it was a huge camp, it became overcrowded as more and more transports arrived. What shocked us on arrival was the appearance of the inmates. The majority were emaciated to the bone, literally walking skeletons—if they were still able to walk. Many were dying: typhus reached epidemic

Basia Brahms,
on the far left,
Miriam's mother,
at Bergen-Belsen.

proportions, starvation took its toll. Whatever food we were given was unfit for consumption. The average life expectancy of an inmate was nine months. By April 1945, thirty-five thousand perished. Yet some prisoners had endured these conditions for years—I can't imagine how. What saved mother and me was the relatively short time of our stay; we were freed by the British army on April 15. Even weeks after our liberation thirteen thousand more died from disease, malnutrition and the effects of torture. Mother and I contracted typhus in April, but gradually recovered.

We were too sick and weak to celebrate our survival; our stomachs found it difficult to adjust to their good fortune and it took weeks to get used to food again. We no longer looked death in the face.
We were free.

To go where? Miriam and her mother were the sole survivors of their decimated family. Freedom from oppression did not result in instant happiness. They mourned their dead, they were scarred from their suffering, and they'd lost five years of their lives. To return to Russian-dominated Kaunas was unthinkable. They had relatives in Canada and Palestine and applied for visas to either of those countries. It happened that their Palestine relatives did business with Sweden and could support their entry to that country; it took a year to be accepted. Miriam and her mother settled in Stockholm. As Miriam writes:

Seated, l. to r., Basia Brahms, mother of Miriam (Brahms) Reich and my Ma, Jennie Reich. Standing, My pa, Harry Reich, Miriam (Ivry) Reich and daughter Harriet Reich, and Sol Ivry.

I started to attend school. It was a regular Swedish school and I entered a year behind to compensate for the six years of formal education that I missed. It was not a happy experience. I didn't understand what the teachers were saying. I had nothing in common with the students and six years with no lessons in mathematics, science or history did not help. Culturally I could have landed on a different planet.

By the end of the school year I could communicate haltingly in Swedish. I also took private English lessons that I really liked. I started reading English books voraciously, looking up almost every word in the dictionary and soon my English improved. When I returned to school I felt like a veteran: I could understand some Swedish, I'd absorbed some algebra and science and could actually keep up with my school work. I also kept plugging away at my English. In December our visas to Canada materialized and again we moved, arriving in Montreal on December 11, 1947.

We stayed with my Aunt Sonia, and in January 1948, I entered Grade Ten of the High School of Montreal. By June I passed all the courses. Of all the languages I spoke, there was not one that I could write correctly or whose grammar I knew. I decided there had to be one language that I could call my own: English. Language is more than a system of communication; it helps forge an identity. By age ten I hadn't absorbed enough of the culture into which I was born, nor knew a language I could call my own. The languages of my childhood represented traces of my past that I wanted to forget. My happy early years had vanished with my home and I wanted a new beginning. I didn't want to be a displaced person forever; in fact, for the first few years I didn't associate with refugees—they brought back unwelcome memories.

It took fifty years for me to deal with the seven painful years I survived. Until I wrote my story, I didn't realize how powerful these memories were. The few pages that I recorded obviously don't tell everything. My recollections appear like a hazy seascape of icebergs floating as far as the eye can see in an enormous ocean. There are clearings through which a late afternoon sun is breaking. Some icebergs are dim, remote and fuzzy, others are near, razor sharp and menacing. But always, much more of their mass is submerged than is visible. To survive, I had to forget many incidents. The human psyche finds ways to protect itself.

Some lived to tell their story, too many did not. I wish there had been no story to tell.

Miriam did arrive at a life free of terror, squalor and hunger. She met Herman Reich; they recognized they were for each other and married on August 29, 1948. Their three children, Robert, Celia and Mark, now successful adults, blessed them with eight grandchildren. Miriam's mother lived with them until her death in 1979.

After fifty-seven happy years together, Herman died in 2006.

Through it all, Miriam never relinquished her quest for education. She completed high school, entered Sir George Williams University, received a Bachelor of Arts degree, and continued at Macdonald College, emerging with a teaching diploma. She taught high school for twenty-three years, enjoying her contact with students, especially the daily challenge of channelling their boundless energy into personal growth and fulfillment. By the end of her career, she'd acquired diplomas for reading instruction and for teaching children with learning disabilities. In 1972 she was awarded

Basia Brahms survived the
Holocaust and reached Montreal.

a Master's Degree in Counselling by McGill University. By filling the lives of others, she fulfilled herself. Miriam concludes her own memoir:

> I think of the six million Jews who were murdered. They never had a chance to fulfill their dreams, nor to pick up their lives as I did. I recall a monument of the Children's Section of Yaad Va'shem, a series of figures standing upright, but incomplete. The upper parts of their bodies are missing, cut off in mid-life. That monument says it all. It applies to all who perished, children and adults alike.

A routine examination disclosed that Miriam suffered from cancer. She fought the disease with the same courage that had always sustained her, but, following a succession of remissions, she succumbed in 2008. Her body had been ravaged but her mind remained intact. She told me two days before she died: "I've had a good life, a fine husband and wonderful children. I've been fortunate." It was a fitting and generous epitaph.

Lisl Epstein Ivry

Lisl Epstein was born in 1925 in the pastoral village of Lichtenstein, nestled amidst lush fields and thick forests in the foothills of Bohemian mountains. Her mother supported her and her brother, younger by two years, by operating one of the four stores that served three hundred townsfolk.

Five generations of her family had passed their lives in what had originally been a small house made of clay mixed with straw; it now belonged to her mother, one of ten children. Sons, when they married, brought their brides to the parents and, when God was good, their babies were born there. As the family grew, so did the home, each addition being readily recognizable by the materials used.

Eventually the building housed living quarters, the family store with a warehouse, a stable, and a chicken coop. There was no plumbing; everyone used an outhouse and water was carried from a neighbouring well each evening. Electricity arrived in 1938; Lisl's childhood was illuminated by petrol lamps. In those innocent days, before radio, television, and other distractions, the family congregated in the large kitchen.

Lisl's father had died before she was four years old and her industrious mother raised the family and operated a general store from her home. It sold everything: cloth, household items, and foods that local farmers didn't produce. Visitors from outlying villages arrived on Sunday mornings, deposited their bags with shopping lists, and attended church. They returned after services to pick up their completed orders, and enjoyed a glass or two of wine served by Lisl in the kitchen.

Those were the happy days. However their idyllic village was located in the Sudetenland, a portion of Czechoslovakia largely inhabited by Germans and claimed by Adolph Hitler. British and French statesmen generously offered it to Germany in return for Adolph Hitler's promise of peace. The world was to learn that Hitler would bring final peace to millions.

In October 1938, the unopposed German army annexed the Sudetenland. Lisl, together with her mother and brother, left with the retreating Czech troops and took refuge with relatives in Prague. In March 1939, the Germans completed their occupation of that helpless nation as the world stood by. Czechoslovakia no longer existed.

The family was trapped.

The new masters lost no time in imposing their will. Jews were subjected to the same treatment described by Miriam Brahms. This was a familiar refrain: wherever Nazis trod, Jews were suppressed, and eventually murdered.

In October 1941, the first transports of Jews from Prague were sent to Lodz, Poland. Lisl's mother and brother were deported to Theresienstadt in August 1942 and she followed the next month.

In the late eighteenth century the Austrian empire had erected a fortress about sixty kilometers north of Prague, named after their empress, Maria Theresa. In peacetime it held about six thousand soldiers; off-season, its walls and readily guarded exits made it a useful prison. The SS and Gestapo adapted it as a holding ghetto to receive Jews and other undesirables destined for extermination. Transports came and went. In addition to Jews from the local population, the ghetto welcomed deportees from Germany, Holland, France, Denmark, and other countries unwilling to allow massacres within their borders. Of one hundred forty-four thousand Jews who enjoyed Theresienstadt's hospitality during the war, thirty-three thousand perished within its walls, eighty-eight thousand were sent to Auschwitz or other extermination camps; about seventeen thousand survived.

The ghetto population included many leading professionals and artists. The SS encouraged concerts, operas, and other entertainments, marred only by unscheduled absences of cast members or orchestra musicians who made their final appearances in the gas chambers of Auschwitz. Part of the ghetto was re-furbished to present a false impression of favourable treatment of its inmates to visiting representatives of the Red Cross. Indeed, this organization looked only at what was shown, and was criticized for giving the Nazis good reports after their inspections.

Lisl and her mother worked in a Theresienstadt hospital until their turn came. Her mother and her brother were transported in September 1943 and Lisl followed in December. Their fate is described in her memoir, *To Hell and Back.*

> On a dark winter's day we were crowded into a cattle car and carried to an unknown destination. The train halted, the doors opened. SS men confronted us with rifles and dogs. They were assisted by men in striped garments; we later learned that they were prisoners conscripted for this work. Carrying what we were able, we were marched to waiting trucks

and driven to what we later learned was Birkenau, an introduction to Auschwitz. Prisoners, conscripted by the SS to assist in herding us, whispered: "Don't get on the trucks. They take you to your death."

We had heard rumours of such unbelievable things, but we had no choice. We were taken to a family camp; men and women were separated, driven to their own camps and locked in barracks. To visit the latrines we lined up, and when ten were assembled, assigned prisoners would accompany us to an outhouse consisting of a concrete floor with holes. A jute cloth divided men from women. A measure of cleanliness was achieved by bathing in long, common troughs. Privacy was a dream.

After two weeks we were allowed to leave the barracks for an hour a week. I learned from a prisoner that my mother was in Block 27 and my brother in Block 18. I was in Block 11, quite distant from my mother. Struggling through ankle-deep mud and losing my wood clogs many times, I reached Block 27. Finding someone among five hundred unkempt, bedraggled women covered with white powder to combat dysentery, was daunting. The prisoners lay eight to a tier, stacked three high. It was dark. I called her name. She crawled out, ill and hungry, in pitiful condition. I had nothing to give her, nothing to ease her suffering.

Next day, I was assigned to carry barrels of soup. The barrels were fitted with poles at their sides and it took two of us stumbling through the mud to transport them. When they had been emptied we were allowed to scrape them; it provided extra food and something I could bring to my mother. It was too late to help her. She had been laid, hardly breathing, with other dying women, and her brave heart gave out January 4, 1944.

We survived the cold winter nights and the freezing dawns when we lined up in rows of five to be counted and re-counted. We constantly ached with hunger and were haunted by the expectation of being selected for the gas chambers. We knew from the numbers tattooed on our arms when each had arrived, and on March 5, 1944, the transport that preceded us in September was taken to the adjoining compound to await death.

The next day I recognized my brother in that group. I was wearing mittens and offered to throw them over the barbed wire to him. He refused: "Where we are going, we don't need mittens."

He was seventeen. I never saw him again. That night we heard singing from the trucks as they were driven to the gas chambers: the Czech and Hebrew national anthems rang through the cold air.

Next morning smoke rose from the crematorium chimneys and a sickly odour fouled the air. All was still. We were left with our thoughts. Mid-May brought a flood of Jewish transports from Hungary. Almost all went directly to the gas chambers and the chimneys belched smoke continuously. We still lived and hoped. Despite our circumstances, we organized an underground organization resolved to fight to the last. What did we have to lose?

We heard that the war was going badly for the German people, and that workers would be needed to clean up their bombed cities. Sure enough, a "selection" was organized and we passed naked before Dr. Mengele who decided who were robust enough for labour. The chosen men and women were marched to new quarters. Other prisoners, jealous because they understood that we would be removed from the camp to work, persecuted us in many petty ways. It was unpleasant, but understandable.

On July 4, 1944, we were again crowded in to cattle cars and left Auschwitz. Few others ever had left alive, but now the Reich needed labourers. The guards accompanying us were not the sadistic SS, but Wermacht. After three days we arrived in Hamburg. We were, for the time being, reprieved. But not free.

The journal stops there, but not her story.

Hamburg was attacked day and night without respite by British and American bombers. Much of the city was destroyed and the task of the prisoners was to clear damage and make building materials for re-construction. Between air raids, Lisl cast concrete blocks in forms and carried bricks. Prisoners were not sheltered and shrapnel from the skies killed many.

As the Russian army advanced into Germany, prisoners were progressively relocated westward through a series of camps. These were arduous moves, made by foot, truck or cattle car. The sick, the crippled or the weak died en route. The survivors' destination was Bergen-Belsen.

Lisl arrived there in February 1945. Originally designed to hold ten thousand inmates, the population swelled to sixty thousand. There were no gas chambers, but an estimated fifty thousand Jews, Czechs, Poles, anti-Nazi Christians, and Gypsies perished there from starvation or disease. After its liberation by British and Canadian troops on April 15, 1945, fifteen thousand more died, many from eating food their systems could no longer digest.

The BBC journalist, Richard Dimbleby, accompanying the troops, reported:

Here over an acre of ground lay dead and dying people. You could not see which was which. The living lay with their heads against the corpses and around them moved the awful, ghostly procession of emaciated, aimless people, with nothing to do and with no hope of life, unable to move out of our way, unable to look at the terrible sights around them. Babies had been born here, tiny, wizened things that could not live. A mother, driven mad, screamed at a British sentry to get milk for her child and thrust the tiny mite into his arms, then ran off crying terribly. He opened the bundle and found the baby had been dead for days. This day in Belsen was the most horrible in my life.

The camp was burned to the ground to stem the typhus epidemic. The war was over. There was no future for her in Czechoslovakia, but she had an uncle in Montreal. He applied for a visa for her; Lisl was to wait four years to receive it. She kept herself occupied studying English and working at a variety of jobs, mostly involving refugees, until she reached what would be her final home in June 1949.

Her uncle owned a beauty parlour. Lisl, having no resources, worked there, but had no interest in becoming a hairdresser or a manicurist. Among her customers were Ma and her sister Miriam. Lisl confided that her talents suited her better to an office and she was recruited for The Store. Sidney, a renowned Moon Brother, was taken with her and on June 25, 1950, they married.

When children didn't appear, they adopted Elsa soon after her birth in 1952. Apparently this stimulated the reproductive process, and Victor was born in 1956. Their families produced five grandchildren. Sidney died in 1996. During her married life, Lisl was not idle. She received a Bachelor of Arts degree from Loyola College, *Magna cum Laude*, honouring in German literature and majoring in Fine Arts. In 1969 she was awarded a diploma in teaching pre-school art, and taught for thirteen years. Today she works as a volunteer at the Holocaust Centre and lectures widely on her experiences. Not many triumphed over Theresienstadt, Auschwitz, and Bergen-Belsen. Lisl did.

PARTING WORDS

I recently donated my architectural records to the *Bibliothèque et Archives Nationale du Québec* and undertook to categorize documents I'd accumulated over more than forty years; another ten years of completed work would stay with the office until it could be released. My agreement required that I sort through two hundred fifty cartons and dispense with superfluous paper: time sheets, invoices, book-keeping, correspondence, abandoned projects—they interested no one. The remaining documents would be sorted and classified as a historical resource. It took four diligent months to separate the meat from the bones, but, when the dust had settled, my life lay stacked in bundles, summarized in the thousands of buildings I'd been involved with, each with its own story. I drew the line and my life entered another phase. I'm relieved of many responsibilities and free to confront my past and, above all, to write it down.

I inherited great gifts from Ma and Pa and regret that I never acknowledged my debt to them. I never felt Pa's pain when he couldn't rescue his family or his anxiety during the years he waited to learn their fate. And I never comforted Ma during her invalid years as she progressively lost her formidable powers.

I never lived up to my potential.

★ ★ ★

That brings me to today. I had always amused my children by inventing stories. While they listened open-mouthed I dropped food into their beaks until I emptied their plates. If they wouldn't sleep I told them tales until their eyelids closed. The little darlings grew up, had kids of their own, and asked what's "The Truth About Ruth

Rottentooth From Duluth?" And what happened to "The Prince and the Blintz?" And where are "The Shlepper and the Donkey?"

I had to admit that they were where they'd always been: in my head. By popular demand I wrote what I remembered and made up the rest. I loved the freedom of creating a world untrammelled by building inspectors, mortgage lenders, and demanding clients. I'm still writing for and about my kids and for those who, God willing, will follow.

Any artistic ability I had manifested itself in sketches that sprang from my fantasies. To the delight of my children and, a generation later, to their offspring, I could transform a calligraphic alphabet into a comedic zoo filled with parodies of animals and humans inhabiting an unbounded universe, one that demanded no apologies or explanations.

I soon realized that adults were only children better able to rationalize their lives and conceal their feelings—I wrote about them. Ten books followed until I undertook these Memoirs. I didn't know Pa's parents, but my grandchildren and their descendants will know me through these pages.

Anyone who has read this far will recognize that good fortune has favoured me more than I deserve. I have been the luckiest man on this planet, and I pray that my children, and theirs, will be as fortunate.

GLOSSARY OF NON-ENGLISH TERMS

Avek tzi di goyim	Gone over to the gentiles
Aktionen	Assemblies in death camps to select Jews destined for extermination
Bal koire	One who reads from the Torah during services celebrating Sabbath or high holidays
Belzer	Follower of the Rabbi of Belze
Boba	Grandmother
Bocher	A young lad
CEGEP	Acronym for Collège d'enseignement général et professionel (College of General and Vocational Education)
Challah	Braided white bread customarily eaten at the Sabbath meal
Chassid (pl: Chassidim)	Member of an Orthodox sect of the Jewish religion
Chazzin	A cantor authorized to chant prayers during services and High Holidays
Cheder	School for teaching reading, writing, religion, and Hebrew to children
Chumash	First five books of the Bible—the Pentateuch
Chutzpah	Nerve, effrontery
Dacha	Summer cottage
Erev	Continuous entity around a community, such as a fence, telephone cable, or railway track, that permits those enclosed within to carry out some activities otherwise forbidden on the Sabbath
Freg nisht	Don't even ask it

Gemora	Commentaries contained in the Talmud
Gimnasium	Pre-university school in Poland and elsewhere, equivalent to college
Golem	Mythological automaton made to resemble a human and given life
Goniff	Thief
Goy (pl: goyim)	Gentile, gentiles
Goyish (adj: goyishe)	Actions, mannerisms, or attitudes attributed to gentiles
Groschen	Small coins
Haggadah	Chronicle of the departure of the Hebrews from Egypt
Judenrein	Cleansed of Jews
Kinde (pl: kinder)	Child, children
Klotz	Clumsy oaf
Kreplach	Small pouches of dough containing meat, potatoes, or cheese
Knaidle (pl: knaidlach)	Small dumpling made of dough
Kosher	Food selected and prepared in accordance with Jewish law
Matzo	Unleavened bread, prepared without yeast
Mishpocha	Extended family
Mittelchock	A cut of beef
Mohel	Cleric authorized to perform circumcisions
Momeh loshen	Mother tongue, usually meaning Yiddish
Mujik	Peasant
Nebech	Deserving of pity
Payes	Earlocks worn by Orthodox Jewish males
Pesach	Passover, the Festival celebrating the departure of the Jews from Egypt
Pesachdik	Item approved for consumption or use on Pesach
Pogrom	Violent anti-Jewish demonstration

Rebbe	Rabbi; title of respect for learned man or teacher
Rebbitzin	Wife of a *Rebbe*
Schnapps	Whiskey
Shadchan	Introduces those seeking marriage partners
Shaigetz, shkotzim	Derogatory designation of non-Jewish boy
Shaitel	Wigs worn by Orthodox Jewish married women
Shiksa	Derogatory term for a non-Jewish female
Shkotzim	See Shaigetz
Shmatta	Rag; uncomplimentary reference to clothing
Shmoozer	One with a predilection for idle chatter
Shochet	Cleric authorized to slaughter animals and fowls in accordance with Jewish law
Shtetl	Village with a significant proportion of Jewish inhabitants
Talmud	Compilation of Jewish laws and commentaries from ancient times
Tihilim	Psalms
Torah	The Pentateuch, the first five Books of the Bible
Yarmulke	Skullcap worn by Jewish males
Yenner velt	The afterlife
Yeshiva	Institution where students study holy books dealing with Jewish laws and customs
Zaida	Grandfather
Zog nisht	Don't even say it

Marquis Book Printing Inc.

Québec, Canada
2010